"In a world that's constantly trying to draw us away from God, Lina points us to the biblical truths we must cling to and believe above all else. What a wonderful resource this book is!"

Lysa TerKeurst, *New York Times* bestselling author and president of Proverbs 31 Ministries

"Jesus told us to come and follow Him. He didn't say it was going to be easy. To do it, we need resolve. I love Lina, and I love this message that is sure to help us break away from a toe-deep, defeated faith to one that rocks our world for Jesus."

Christine Caine, author of *Undaunted* and cofounder of the A21 Campaign

"There are some people who write books that make you want to grab a Snuggie and cuddle. But Lina isn't one of those writers. She is skilled at drawing out the warrior in her readers and motivating them to be resolved in following Jesus. In *Resolved*, she challenges us to make a decision and includes simple ways to work out our commitment."

Bianca Juarez Olthoff, preacher, teacher, and Chief Storyteller for A21

"*Resolved* is an immensely practical and helpful book. It addresses both the temptations we commonly face and the biblical principles we need for courageous, uncompromising obedience. It teaches us to abandon fear and live for the ultimate glory of the God who is resolved to love us. I'm glad to have read it and now recommend it."

Jen Pollock Michel, author of *Teach Us to Want*

"Cultural Christianity promises the 'good life,' but authentic Christian faith remembers the words of Jesus: 'In this world you will have trouble.' Dr. Lina AbuJamra challenges us to live out our faith in the real world when things do not go as we wish. 'Follow me' is still the call of Christ. Anything less is not worthy of the name *Christian*."

Gary D. Chapman, PhD, author of *The Five Love Languages* and *Love As a Way of Life*

"Lina lives what she writes, and I'm grateful for her open heart and clear voice in the matter of us becoming strong men and women of faith. Every push she gives throughout the book will bring glory to God and good to our lives. I can't imagine someone reading this and not being changed—for the better, for good."

Annie F. Downs, author of *Let's All Be Brave*

"Following Jesus seems like an intriguing invitation . . . until you hear Him say, 'Take up my cross and follow Me.' It's the challenging aspects of following Christ that seems so daunting and so hard to navigate, and often end up derailing the most wonderful journey of life. Thanks to my friend Lina, we now have some relevant and solid advice for how to follow Christ regardless."

Dr. Joseph M. Stowell, president of Cornerstone University

"My dear friend Lina is brilliant, candid, engaging, and loves Jesus with obvious abandon—I like to think of her as a modern-day chick version of the apostle Paul! She writes about our Creator-Redeemer with such contagious passion and refreshing authenticity that you're bound to see Him 'bigger' as a result!"

Lisa Harper, author and Bible teacher

"*Resolved* is spiritual medicine lovingly prescribed by a real-life ER doctor. Dr. Lina AbuJamra is a pediatrician and Bible teacher who gives us chewable pills that taste like candy and who somehow makes us laugh when it's time for her to fill her syringe and give us a shot of truth that helps us, as believers, to get well. She reminds us of what it means to be a Christian and she makes Bible stories super fun to hear. Every chapter in this book needs to be shouted from the rooftops. If for no other reason, Christians should buy this book just to memorize and apply its table of contents. It's a book that makes you feel clean after you read it."

Sarah Sumner, PhD, MBA, founder of Right On Mission
and author of Angry Like Jesus

"*Resolved* is precisely what you need from an ER doctor: a direct assessment and clear prescription for life—and life in Jesus. It asks questions designed to provide healing solutions. It doesn't mess around with small talk but uses Scripture to make its life-giving point. Lina Abujamra takes a verbal scalpel to the root of the things that infect and weaken our lives. She has the profound gift of combining a startling vulnerability with eternal truth in succinct language. I was deeply moved and greatly helped!"

Richard Foth, coauthor with Mark Batterson of A Trip Around
the Sun: Turning Your Everyday Life into the Adventure of a Lifetime

"*Resolved* applies Scripture practically and includes transparent experiences from Lina's life, offering a friend you can trust for the journey. I've always appreciated Lina's earnest commitment to Christ and His Word, so if you're looking for solid, honest, biblically based encouragement, this book is for you."

Kelly Minter, Bible teacher and author of What Love Is: A Study
on 1, 2 & 3 John

"Lina AbuJamra mentors us through the deepest questions we face. Yes, we've absolutely discovered that Jesus is the real deal. We've taken risks of faith and He's come through for us. We've found a kind of encouragement and joy we hadn't known to look for. But now we've been at this for a while and that early glow has faded. What does it look like, in the face of real disappointments, to follow that most profound spiritual advice of all: *Hang in there!* Lina is the best type of coach, full of empathy and yet tough and unyielding that our only path is forward."

Dave Schmelzer, executive director of Blue Ocean Faith and author
of Not the Religious Type: Confessions of a Turncoat Atheist

"I'm impressed by Lina AbuJamra. I'm impressed by her energy and intelligence; I'm impressed by her openness and authenticity. But most of all I'm impressed by the depth of her commitment to following Jesus. This is what stands out in her wonderful book, *Resolved*. Drawing upon Scripture and her own experience, Lina shows us what it looks like to be a serious disciple of Jesus in the twenty-first century. I'm certain this book is going to help many others find new resolve to radically follow Jesus."

Brian Zahnd, lead pastor of Word of Life Church, St. Joseph, Missouri,
and author of A Farewell to Mars

RESOLVED

10 Ways to Stand Strong and Live
What You Believe

LINA
ABUJAMRA

BakerBooks

a division of Baker Publishing Group
Grand Rapids, Michigan

Published by Baker Books
a division of Baker Publishing Group
P.O. Box 6287, Grand Rapids, MI 49516–6287
www.bakerbooks.com

Printed in the United States of America

Library of Congress Cataloging-in-Publication Data
Names: AbuJamra, Lina, author.
Title: Resolved : 10 ways to stand strong and live what you believe / Lina
    AbuJamra.
Description: Grand Rapids, MI : Baker Books, 2016.
Identifiers: LCCN 2015043708 | ISBN 9780801006524 (pbk.)
Subjects: LCSH: Christian life.
Classification: LCC BV4501.3 .A25 2016 | DDC 248.4—dc23 LC record
    available at http://lccn.loc.gov/2015043708

Published in association with the literary agency of Credo Communications, LLC, Grand Rapids, Michigan 49525; www.credocommunications.net.

17 18 19 20 21 22   8 7 6 5 4 3

For Diana,
whose resolve to be like Jesus
continues to fuel my own.

Contents

Acknowledgments

Some books are easier to write than others. In this case, I know it's only because of the brilliant support of these folks:

Brian Thomasson, my editor at Baker Books. Thank you. You saw the finished product before its inception and helped shape it into its present form. I am so thankful for your vision and faith in me. Also, thanks to the entire team at Baker Books who have worked so hard with me, especially Lindsey Spoolstra, Ruth Anderson, and Hannah Brinks.

Special thanks to Tim Beals and the folks at Credo Communications, and to Karen Campbell of Karen Campbell Media.

I continue to be deeply thankful for my team at Living with Power Ministries: Bonnie, Tina, Nate, Diana, and Rafi. I am deeply thankful for your loyalty and patience.

I am indebted to my Pediatric ER friends and colleagues. You guys make it possible for me to fulfill God's calling on my life. Thank you.

I am blown away by the kindness of brothers and sisters in Christ who still read my blog and watch my Bible studies and send me emails telling me how God is working in their lives. I wouldn't be doing what I'm doing without you.

Thanks to those who have trusted me to teach in their churches and colleges and conferences and retreats. My life is fuller because of you.

Finally, thanks to my mom and dad, whose unconditional love allows me to risk without fear of crashing. Thanks to Nick, Patricia, Maya, Leya, Fawzi, Ramzi, and Rafi. Thanks to my own personal entourage and posse of personal advisors: Diana, Ben, Micah, and Samuel.

I saved the best for last: Jesus. You're the reason I do what I do. You're the One I worship and adore. May every breath that I take bring You praise. I'll never get over Your love for me. Thank You barely scratches the surface of what I feel for You, but it's a start.

Introduction

It Starts Right Now

Resolved [ri-zolvd]
Adjective
Firm in purpose or intent; determined.

I remember a time in my life when I felt like I was sinking—and fast. During that season, I finally got to a point where I had no choice but to throw it all at God: my sin, my pride, my lust, my hurt, my dreams, my hopes, my gifts, my all. I found that it didn't matter what I threw at God, He was never shocked by it. He was never mad. He didn't avoid me or push me away. Instead, He walked with me through my pain and showed me a better way. It is usually in the painful seasons of our lives that we learn who God really is and what He longs to do in us and through us. It is in our darkest places that we sense His love for us, a love that remains near even when no one else can stand to.

Jesus was a master at asking the right questions. One day a blind beggar named Bartimaeus came up to Jesus wanting to be healed. "Have mercy on me," he said. In response, Jesus looked at Bartimaeus and asked, "What do you want me to do for you?" (Mark 10:46–52).

That's a great question to ask at the beginning of this road together. Why don't you try answering it right now? What is it that you want from God? What do you need Him to do in your life? The only way to answer the question is to understand where you're at today. What's your problem? Are you alive? Do you feel alive? How's your connection to the power source of life? Is there a disconnect somewhere?

I'm a kids' ER doctor in my day job. There's a phenomenon in resuscitation that we call pulseless electrical activity (PEA). It's where the patient has a heart rhythm but no definite pulse. It's confusing for everyone involved in the resuscitation. Is the patient dead or alive? In principle, the patient is alive but somewhere deep inside them is a significant problem that will ultimately lead to cardiac arrest and death if not corrected.

We are facing an epidemic in the church today. There is a deep disconnect between what Christians say we believe and how we live, and it's threatening to destroy us. We say we believe in a God who rose from the dead but we live with a steady sense of defeat. We know we should have joy but walk around in a haze of worry. We say God can do anything but we don't believe He will do anything for us. Despite years of faith under our belts, all it takes is one small trial to topple the most seasoned Christian into a place of despair. We are weak and quickly shaken, leaving the watching world underwhelmed by us. Maybe that describes you too. You long to bridge the gap between what you say you believe and how you live. You look alive but you feel dead. You're not even sure what your problem is. But you'd like to find out. You want to stand strong in the heat of the battle. You're tired of feeling like your faith is only toe-deep.

What you need, whether or not you know it, is *resolve*. It's a word dreams are made of. It's a word that's changed the course of many people's lives. You resolved to open this book and read it. Congratulations. Your life is about to change.

Or you might have picked up this book because something feels amiss with your life. You're not happy. You're not fulfilled. You're tired of feeling wishy-washy. You want your life to be different, more impactful. You need help and you want to fix the problem. Good. You're going to get some answers by the end of our time together.

Maybe you picked up this book but you're skeptical. You feel like you've been there and tried that but it simply hasn't worked. Every resolve you've ever made has failed, so why try again? What guarantee do you have of succeeding this time? Many of us confuse living by resolve with the tradition of making New Year's resolutions. Did you know that almost half of Americans set New Year's resolutions but only 8 percent are successful?

Think back to the last time you made a New Year's resolution. You were so convinced you were going to lose those ten extra pounds. You really believed you were going to take advantage of that gym membership. You were so sure you were going to keep up with that Bible reading plan, build up that savings account, and stop buying those things on Amazon that you never really needed. And in every single scenario, your resolution barely lasted a month. So you opened this book with a natural guardedness. I don't blame you.

The problem with so many of the resolutions we make is that they don't really matter in the big scheme of life. They feel important in the moment, but when push comes to shove it's easy to ignore them. I mean, who really cares if you buy yet another pair of shoes you don't really need? Furthermore, most resolutions we make tend to be motivated by guilt or fear. *Will I ever get married if I don't lose that weight? What will happen to me if I face a crisis without a financial cushion?*

What I'm going to do in the following pages is show you what true biblical resolve looks like. We're going to talk about the kind of resolve that's impossible to accomplish on our own. It is the kind of resolve that is motivated by a changed life and a transformed heart that longs to please and glorify God. Instead of focusing on what we're missing out on in life, we're going to fix our eyes on all that is gained when we live our lives with godly resolve. The good news is that we're not in this alone. Our God is a God of resolve. He's resolved to love us without limit. He's resolved to stay with us no matter what. He's resolved to give us everything we need to live an abundant life.

As the years have passed and I've gotten older, I've noticed that I can get caught up in living my life without really feeling alive. I catch myself going through the motions. As a Christian, a follower of Jesus Christ, I notice that I talk about God. I say I know Him. I reiterate that I believe in His resurrection power. But too often my life simply doesn't reflect it. I know *what* I'm supposed to be doing and I have enough motivation to do it, but I catch myself failing to follow through. When my life gets hard and feels out of control, all my good intentions go out the window and I become discouraged and afraid. I'm tempted to give up.

Have you ever felt this way?

No matter how strong we claim our faith in God is, when life is hard it all comes down to resolve. Do we really believe what we say we believe? The answer we come up with not only affects our feelings but also our culture. Going through the motions is a dangerous place to live for followers of Jesus Christ.

We are living in an age where there is much at stake in our obedience. We are called to be the light of the world, the salt of the earth. We are to stick out in a culture that is desperately looking for answers. If we don't figure out this thing we call the Christian life, and live like we mean it, we will be thrown out and trampled under people's feet.

I don't want to be trampled. I want my life to declare that God is real and alive and powerful and risen from the dead. I know you want that too.

In the following pages I'm going to present ten resolutions that every follower of Jesus Christ must make in order to stand strong in the shifting sands of our culture. I hope to help you understand the disconnect between what we say we believe and how we live. I want to give you biblical strategies for lasting change that will allow you to stand strong no matter what.

Until you get to the place in your life where you see your need for change, you'll never change. Our world is changing. Our culture has blurred the lines when it comes to truth. Christians have become adept at bending God's Word to suit the cultural flavor of the day. Think about it: Whose definition of marriage have you adopted? Does life really begin at conception? Could the world really have been created in just six days? It's easy to feel the pressure to compromise and give in to the popular beliefs of whatever fad everyone is trying to grab on to. The only way to stay strong in a shifting culture is to resolve to know God and live by His truth. The greatest platform you and I have is how we respond when our lives are shaken by trial. If God's Word is true, then the followers of Jesus Christ ought to be the happiest and strongest people on the planet.

But it all starts with resolve. Are you resolved to do whatever it takes to become the kind of Christian God has called you to be? Are you resolved to change no matter how uncomfortable it might be? You're about to be challenged in ten critical areas of your life. In each of these areas, you're going to have to decide whether you're willing to live by the truth or not. If you're longing to make a difference in your world, you don't really have a choice. You simply must do this. Now let's get moving and talk about the first resolution we must make in order to stand strong in the shifting sands of our culture.

1

Believe When
It Looks Ridiculous

You might remember the first time you turned to Jesus for healing. You thought your life would be awesome. You thought you could do anything with God at your side. He had died and risen again for you. Nothing could stop you from believing that God was going to come through for you. Then one day . . .

The waters got too high, the storms too strong.

You looked for immediate relief and didn't find it.

You had a question but didn't get the answer you were looking for.

You wanted a specific solution and didn't get it.

You felt cheated.

Your expectations were crushed.

Your hopes were deflated.

Your dreams were put on hold.

Your life plan didn't turn out as you intended it to, and here you are. All the self-help and personal coaching in the world haven't plugged the void in your life. All the sermons you can listen to and Bible studies you attend aren't helping bridge the gap you sense between what you say you believe and how you live. All the blogs in the world aren't giving you the answers that your heart longs for. You're dissatisfied, frustrated, less than alive. You feel betrayed by the unexpected, disillusioned by your faith.

This is the life of power you were told you'd receive? *This* is the abundant life with Jesus?

In John 10:10, Jesus told His disciples: "The thief comes only in order to steal and kill and destroy. I came that they may have and enjoy life, and have it in abundance [to the full, till it overflows]" (AMP).

Abundant. Powerful. Overflowing. That's supposed to be the destiny of every follower of Jesus Christ. Yet . . . for most of us who call ourselves Christians, our lives don't demonstrate the truth of these verses. Something is desperately wrong. If God has far more for our lives than we can imagine, it's time we grab hold of the truth and run.

When I was eight years old I had severe abdominal pain. My parents waited for three days before taking me to the doctor. I almost died, but I promise I'm not holding it against them. I had an infection in my gut and we didn't know why. When we got to the hospital, all we could do was hope that we had found the right physician, and then I had to put my life in his care—completely. I had to let go and entrust my life to the physician's hands.

When it comes to our Christian life, we have been given more than just hope. We've been given a resurrected Savior. He died for us and He lives to give us hope. He asks for our trust—daily. You probably had no trouble giving Him this kind of trust early on. Do you remember when you first realized that you were a sinner in need of God's grace? You believed God's Word. You entrusted your eternal life into His outstretched arms. You gave Him your all—at least for a while, until things started to get complicated.

Believing God when life is smooth is easy. It's when we're in the midst of the storm that the true nature of our faith is revealed. The disciples were busted for their weak faith every time a storm hit. Even though they had witnessed the amazing power of Jesus over and over again, all it took were a few waves for their true colors to show. And over and over again, Jesus lovingly rebuked the disciples with these words: "You of little faith, why did you doubt?" Unless we resolve to believe God no matter what, we will sink in a culture that challenges our faith with its pressing circumstances: unexpected illnesses, unforeseen disasters, unfair attacks by those we thought were our friends, uncompromising schedules, trials that have no end, prayers that remain unanswered, problems without obvious solutions. The list is endless. Which of these pressing circumstances is threatening to undo you? You long to believe God no matter what but can't seem to pull it off in the fury of the storm.

How do we go from simply talking about trusting God with the details of our lives to actually living it out, victoriously, one challenge at a time? Do we have to believe God first and then see how things play out, or does God show up first and our faith follows?

He Believed God

They say "repetition is the mother of learning," which is why even though you're probably very familiar with the story of David and Goliath, I'd like to revisit it. Like a river you've fished at a million times before but can't help going back to and loving for its familiarity, the story of David and Goliath still has the ability to inspire me to a faith that is deeper and stronger than I currently have. Goliath was big and scary and immovable and overwhelming. And he was very real. To make matters worse, Goliath hated the people of Israel. On that particular day Goliath challenged the entire army of Israel and, understandably, they were petrified. They reacted predictably. Here's what happened: "When Saul and all Israel heard these words of the Philistine, they were dismayed and greatly afraid" (1 Sam. 17:11).

Duh. Of course they were afraid. The giant was big and the people couldn't see past him. They panicked. They needed a miracle. Instead, God sent them an unexpected deliverer, someone they never saw coming. God sent them a young man named David.

Young David, the future king, was the runt of the eight sons of Jesse. He was a keeper of sheep who liked to sing and write poetry. He was often overlooked in a home full of muscles and testosterone. The day Samuel showed up to anoint the next king of Israel, no one even remembered that little David was out in the field—except for God. But that's a story for another time.

The morning David faced his Goliath he had been assigned a chore, and a simple chore at that. His father Jesse had given him a sack lunch to take to his brothers who were face-to-face with Goliath at the Valley of Elah. David faithfully did what his father had asked him to do, even though I imagine he must have felt like the new kid on the block, a little wet behind the ears compared to his mighty warrior brothers. But David didn't let any dormant fears get the best of him, and pretty soon he got caught up in the action. The sack lunch was forgotten and the drama of the moment took over.

All the men of Israel, when they saw the man, fled from him and were much afraid. And the men of

Israel said, "Have you seen this man who has come up? Surely he has come up to defy Israel. And the king will enrich the man who kills him with great riches and will give him his daughter and make his father's house free in Israel." And David said to the men who stood by him, "What shall be done for the man who kills this Philistine and takes away the reproach from Israel? For who is this uncircumcised Philistine, that he should defy the armies of the living God?" (1 Sam. 17:24–26)

All the other men of Israel cowered in disbelief while David stood strong in faith and resolved in focus. What made David so different than everyone around him? What allowed him to stand strong when everyone else wobbled? How did David practice God's peace while everyone else fretted? Talk about impacting your culture. We're told that after the battle against Goliath no one could stop talking about David and his God. They even wrote songs about it.

There's an incredible truth for us in David's story that we can't afford to miss if we have any hope of standing strong in the shifting sands of our culture. It's a truth that's life changing and empowering, and it's simpler than you might imagine.

What we believe when we're facing our giants will determine how we act.

The problem with most giants is that they make us feel afraid. They rob us of our joy and shake the very foundations of our faith, mainly because they're so big. And only a God-given resolve can turn our attention away from our giants and fix our eyes on Jesus.

What ridiculously large and imposing giant are you facing in your life today? What is your river you think is uncrossable? Is it a marriage you've given up on? Is it a financial mess you can't straighten out? Is it a job you can't land or a love you can't find? Is it a sin that's so big you can't see around it? Or is it a dream you can't move? What is the giant in your life that has you in a headlock? If you long for victory over it, you need to understand that where you fix your eyes when you're up against the giant has a far greater impact on how you live, what you feel, and how you react.

I'm talking about your faith.

I'm talking about not being conformed to this world but being transformed by the renewing of your mind (Rom. 12:1–2).

I'm talking about setting your mind on heavenly things and not on the things of this world. You can either focus your mind on your giant or you can focus your attention on God. Like David's brothers, most of us have become incredibly adept at fixing our eyes on the obvious giants in our lives. It's not hard to do. Our giants are huge and they're real. Like David's brothers, we might even resent the Davids in our lives. They upset and threaten us. They don't inspire us. They make us feel peeved. When Eliab, David's oldest brother, saw David's courage, he said, "Why have you come down? And with whom have you left those few sheep in the wilderness? I know your presumption and the evil of your heart, for you have come down to see the battle" (1 Sam. 17:28).

Insecurity has a way of bringing out the worst in us. It's easy to deflect the attention away from our own fears and insecurities by attacking those around us. But David remained undeterred, undaunted, and unshaken. His eyes were nowhere near the giant standing before him. His eyes were fixed on the Lord. Saul, the king of Israel, was shocked. How in heaven's name could this kid take on a giant like Goliath? But David's focus couldn't have been clearer.

> "Your servant used to keep sheep for his father. And when there came a lion, or a bear, and took a lamb from the flock, I went after him and struck him and delivered it out of his mouth. And if he arose against me, I caught him by his beard and struck him and killed him. Your servant has struck down both lions and bears, and this uncircumcised Philistine shall be like one of them, for he has defied the armies of the living God." And David said, "The LORD who delivered me from the paw of the lion and from the paw of the bear will deliver me from the hand of the Philistine." (vv. 34–37)

We can't afford to miss it: even before facing Goliath, David had already won the battle of belief in the secret places of his heart. Years before facing his giant, David had learned that the secret to winning every battle was to train his eyes on his Lord.

David believed God. That was his secret.

I've heard faith described as believing God's Word and acting on it no matter how we feel, knowing that God promises a good result. David had experienced this life-altering truth, and when given the chance to show his faith in the face of his giant, David simply practiced his belief that God was his ever-faithful and never-changing deliverer.

Unless we resolve to believe God not just for our salvation but also for our everyday practical life, we will sink in a culture that continuously challenges us to fear and panic and fall into despair. God does care about every little detail of our lives. Whether you live in Chicago or Paducah, God cares about the details of your life. He cares about your newborn's feeding issues or the fact that you're still single. He cares about your unexpected car bill and your respiratory infection. I guarantee you He cares, because of the life of Jesus. After spending hours ministering to people and healing their diseases, Jesus spent as much time making sure they had a meal to eat before going home in the dark. No problem is too minor for God. He's not just a Savior for later on, in eternity. He's your Savior and Provider right now. You can bother God with the mundane. If anyone understands how tedious everyday life can get, it's Jesus. Don't settle for less than the abundant life God has promised you! Don't let anything obscure your vision.

The Trouble with Specks

So much of our faith in God has to do with where we determine to fix our eyes when faced with life's challenging circumstances. In principle, it shouldn't be difficult to fix our eyes on Jesus. We believe the gospel message, after all. That God sent His Son Jesus to live a perfect life and die for us seems to be a completely trustworthy fact. That He was crucified for us and that He rose again after three days is pure truth to our ears. That He is seated at the right hand of God making intercession for us, that He lives in us and has a purpose for us, and that He loves us unconditionally all sound great. But what looks easy on paper becomes impossible when the giants in our lives distort our vision.

I recently took care of a kid who came into the ER because of eye pain. I examined the eye and couldn't find the problem. I placed a fluorescein drop in the eye to check for corneal abrasions but came up empty. Eventually, I looked under the upper eyelid and finally found the culprit: a 1 mm speck of dirt had lodged itself underneath the eyelid. I took a Q-tip and dabbed it out. The kid expressed immediate relief. It has always surprised me that a tiny speck can cause so much pain and discomfort. It doesn't take more than a speck to distort one's vision in life. Many of us are looking for boulders to overcome for the victorious life of faith while all the while it is the tiny specks in our lives that cause us the most pain. Most specks we face come in one of three different forms.

1. The Speck of Distraction

Do you text and drive? Many people think they can look away from the road for a split second and be okay. They are wrong. Before they know it they find themselves in my ER, staring up at my smiling face from their gurney. We are living in the age of distractions. Few tasks are completed without an intermittent buzz from an unwanted phone call or the pesky demands of the urgent.

It's time to lay aside the urgent for the sake of the important, and nothing is more important than learning to fix our eyes on Jesus. Are you prioritizing your time in God's Word? Do you make it a habit to spend time in prayer? How sacred is your time with Jesus? Do you cut it short to make it to your yoga class on time? Do you skip it because the kids are off of school? It's easy to tell yourself you'll squeeze Jesus in later, but it never works. Fixing your eyes on Jesus must be an intentional priority in your life. David spent hours out in the fields with the sheep with his eyes fixed on the Lord. He wrote songs to God. He thought about God. He rejoiced in God's character and meditated on God's truths. It paid off when the going got tough.

Most of us think we're too busy to be bothered with time alone with God. My father is on kidney dialysis. Three times a week he takes four hours out of his schedule to sit in a chair and wait for his blood to be cycled through the machine. Without it, he'd be dead. It's amazing how quickly we can find twelve hours a week to sit in a chair and do nothing when our lives depend on it. We say we need the Lord daily. We believe it to be critical to our spiritual health, but the way we spend our time hardly reflects the honest nature of our belief regarding our time with God. If God's Word is food for our soul and sweeter than the honeycomb, if God's Word is light to our path, then we've got to develop some habits that will strengthen our spiritual health. If we believe time with the Lord daily is life-changing, then we must not allow the little specks of distractions to rob us of such a life-giving practice.

2. The Speck of Defeat

Defeat has a way of killing our faith.

I used to hate failure but I'm learning to appreciate it. I'm learning that failure is never final, and with God it is always meant for our good. If you're alive right now the odds are you've faced defeat at some point in your life—even if it was back with your little league baseball team. When up against our own inadequacies, we are tempted to give up. But did you know that God isn't surprised by our failures? He's the One who fearfully and wonderfully made us and knitted us in our mother's womb (Ps. 139:13–14). He remembers that we are dust (Ps. 103:14). He knows exactly where to find us when we're dealing with the speck of failure in our lives.

David may have felt like a failure when his brothers dressed for war and he was left home alone tending the sheep. David may have felt like a failure when he was given the simple job of packing brown-bag lunches for the real men out there. But it was David's humility in the face of his own insecurities that became the pathway to his promotion. Breakthrough is what happens when we keep on doing what we're supposed to be doing even if nobody notices. Breakthrough is what we experience when we resolve to obey God one day at a time even if we can't see the outcome.

Adoniram Judson is one of the greatest missionaries of all time. He spent his life in Burma preaching the gospel of Jesus Christ. He had one convert in his first year on the mission field. He had only eighteen followers of Jesus after ten years of service. He suffered personal tragedy after tragedy, losing his kids and his wife, and could have quit. I might have quit. But Adoniram Judson did not. He could have assumed defeat, but he understood that God was bigger than his seeming failures. God's plans are never hindered by our defeat. His grace is our strength in our weakness, and His mercy is our hope at the beginning of each new day. Today the largest Christian force in Burma (Myanmar) is the Burma Baptist Convention, which owes its origin to Adoniram Judson. It boasts over 600,000 members in over 3,700 congregations. We must refuse to let our failures deter us from our mission. It's time we see in our defeat the opportunity to run to Jesus. The tiny speck of defeat is a comma, not a period—a pause on the way to victory.

3. The Speck of Delay

Most of us are flummoxed by delays. We don't understand why we must wait so long. You might be single and sick of waiting for "the one." You might be married and still waiting for a child. You might be waiting for a job, a promotion, your graduation, or your turn at the restaurant. No matter the location, at the mere sight of a waiting room most of us break into hives and threaten to jump ship. *Is God really here?* we ask ourselves. *Has He forgotten about me?* Gone is the strong faith that was ours when we first turned to Jesus. Gone is the gratitude we felt at the mere sight of God's grace. How soon we forget that God's delays are not His denials. Just because we haven't seen it happen yet doesn't mean it's not going to happen. Trusting God means believing not only that He will do what He has said He will do but that He will do it in His perfect timing.

Too many Christians are blinded by the waiting room. They begin to question God and His goodness.

It would have been easy for David to doubt God at the Valley of Elah. Here was a guy who had already been anointed king but was still watching sheep as a day job. He could have wondered why God had delayed in fulfilling His promise. He could have blamed God for not doing what He had promised. But David didn't. David saw in the delay an opportunity to grow in his faith and build a history with God. In fact, David's waiting season was far from over. Just because he beat Goliath in the Valley of Elah didn't mean his life was about to be problem-free. David's problems were just getting started. Fortunately for David, his eyes weren't fixed on his problems but on his God.

Do you feel stalled by the tiny speck of delay in your life? Instead of focusing on the delay, focus on building your history with God so that you have something to fix your eyes on the next time you face a Goliath that is even bigger than the one staring at you right now.

What we focus on and where we fix our minds determines how we live and what we feel. If we're looking for the life that's unshaken, it's time to look past our giants and fix our eyes and our minds on Jesus.

Speaking of Jesus

Just like Goliath at the Valley of Elah, our giants can fall in a New York minute. What seems impossible for us right now can fade into oblivion as God becomes big and our circumstances shrink. It's all a matter of recognizing three basic principles about Jesus, the perfect Son of God.

1. His Promises Are Surer Than Our Feelings

If you're one of those people who tend to lean more heavily on your feelings when it comes to God's presence in your life, you're setting yourself up for failure. One of my favorite Bible passages is penned by Job, a man who endured more trials than any one person ever should. He said:

> Behold, I go forward, but he is not there,
> and backward, but I do not perceive him;
> on the left hand when he is working, I do not
> behold him;
> he turns to the right hand, but I do not see
> him.
> But he knows the way that I take;
> when he has tried me, I shall come out as
> gold. (Job 23:8–10)

Job's problem was that when things got really hard in his life, he stopped feeling God's presence. No more goose bumps. No easy answers. No magic pills to swallow. For Job, when things looked really grim, the only security he had was the security of God's promises through His Word. If you're aiming for a touchy-feely kind of Holy Spirit experience to help you recognize God's presence in your life, you need to face up to the fact that the Holy Spirit is much, much more than a feeling.

We need to move past the high we get during Sunday morning song time and live in the daily joy of the certainty of God's presence. We must stop relying on our senses to spot God's presence in our lives. Our stability doesn't emanate from our feelings but from the very real fact of God's presence and the promise of His faithfulness. What God has promised, He *will* accomplish. What God has spoken *will* come to pass. David understood it when the winds blew strong in the Valley of Elah, and so must we.

As I write this chapter, my father is dying. Each time the phone rings I feel the winds blowing over my heart as it plummets. Will this be the call? The worry threatens to squeeze the life out of me. Whatever your circumstances may be today, you know how quickly life can change. And so do our feelings—they change like the wind. The only thing that remains forever, a sure and steadfast anchor for our soul, is God's unchanging Word. If you want to stand unshaken in the heat of your battle, it's time to recognize how erratic our feelings can be and settle on the sure foundation of the living Word of God.

2. His Purposes Are Always for Our Good

It doesn't always feel like it, does it? Yet there's power in looking in the rearview mirror and learning from our lions and our bears. Shortly after I published my first book I became a little bit depressed. My dream had been to become an overnight sensation, a major league MVP for Jesus, but instead, I felt like a little league player. Would I ever publish another book if my first one didn't sell enough copies? Would I ever have a future in ministry if my book sales were just average? I was so overwhelmed by the giant of perceived failure and so caught up in what I wanted God to do in my life that I missed what God had already done. I already had my "lion and bear" story but I hadn't paid any attention to it. It was time for me to take the patches off my eyes and see. God wasn't waiting for me to have a big literary breakthrough to use me in ministry. God's willingness to use me in ministry to impact my world was never based on who I am but had always been because of His own greatness and His grace. Because I had been there and done that, I could now face the future with confidence.

Are you blind when it comes to seeing God at work in your life? Are you overlooking the awesomeness of the great works He has already accomplished in your life? It might be time to sit down and take the patches off your eyes. God's promise to those who love Him and are called according to His purpose is that all things will work out together for our good. The God who helped us back when we were facing the lion and the bear is the same God who is helping us take down Goliath today. His purposes are always for our good, even when we don't understand them. His purposes are for our good even when we don't know how they will ever happen. His purposes are for our good even when the outcome doesn't look in our favor right now.

David was given armor to wear against Goliath but quickly removed it. He understood that the outcome of the battle had little to do with his own abilities and everything to do with God's purpose for his life. In David's case, victory over Goliath came quickly. In your life and mine, the victory isn't always immediate. It's tempting to doubt God's goodness when our circumstances don't match what we think is "our good." My life verse is Philippians 1:6. It says, "And I am sure of this, that he who began a good work in you will bring it to completion at the day of Jesus Christ." I'm learning not to judge God too soon. The verdict on your specific circumstances and mine might not be in yet, but what we can be sure of is God's character: He is always good. He's a God worthy of our trust. He's a God who always finishes what He starts.

3. His Faithfulness Is Greater Than Our Failures

If you're looking too closely at your giant, it's time to step back and get ahold of the bigger picture. It's time to look past your giant. Most of us think too small. Our dreams are too narrow and revolve primarily around us. God is always doing much more than we see. He is always building a bigger kingdom and seeking a higher end point. The goal at the Valley of Elah wasn't simply about a kid from the sticks defeating a giant named Goliath. This wasn't about David becoming a superhero. God's goal was bigger. God's goal was the protection and salvation of the people of Israel. God's goal was the eventual birth of a man named Jesus of the line of David. God's goal was ultimately the salvation of the whole world, including you and me. God used David as a perfect picture of Jesus Christ stepping into our battles, facing our giants, and winning our victories for us, an eternal reminder that we are free to step aside and let Him win our battles for us daily. Have you discounted God's faithfulness in your life? Are you judging Him by your present circumstances?

In 2 Timothy 2:13 God promises that, "If we are faithless, he remains faithful." God's promised faithfulness stands true not just when we accidentally fail but also when we cause our own failures with our self-focused decisions. Whenever I'm stuck in the rut of sinful choices, I think about Samson. This guy had it all. He was chosen by God, he had godly parents, and he was physically able and strong. Yet Samson blew it over and over again. He married the wrong girl(s). He made bad friends, and eventually he suffered for his dumb decisions. His eyes were plucked out and he was thrown into prison. If anyone deserved his punishment, Samson did. Yet God in His mercy still faithfully used Samson in an epic way to defeat the Philistines one last time before his death. If we are faithless, God still somehow remains faithful to the end. Only time will reveal the bigger picture of God's faithfulness toward you. Life with God is far better than you ever dared imagine. God is building His kingdom, and He is using you to help in the process.

David could have stood on the sidelines with his brothers, staring at Goliath in disbelief. Thank God he didn't. Instead David refused to succumb to the pressure of fixing his mind on what everyone else was focused on. God used David to change the world as a result of his unwavering resolve to believe God when it looked ridiculous.

Nothing will destroy our impact faster than settling for the same kind of faith that many others in today's culture are going for, a me-centered, prosperity-driven, blessings-focused, comfort-seeking kind of faith. It's a faith that judges God by how many houses He gives us and how happy He makes us. Alternatively, the kind of faith that will allow us to shine brightly is the kind of faith that is rooted in God's character and the truth of His promises. It doesn't shift when the going gets tough. It is able to withstand occasional delays and the sense of personal failure. It's a faith that rests in the finished work of Jesus Christ and glories in the sure victory that is ours in Him.

As followers of Jesus Christ, we believe a whole lot of crazy stuff. We believe in a Triune God. We believe in the virgin birth. We believe in the resurrection. We believe in the Holy Spirit. We believe in eternal life. If we're honest about it, the story of Jesus is either the craziest story ever told or it's worth giving everything up for, including our fears.

Isn't it time we resolve to believe that God can handle whatever trials and giants come our way? If we long to make a difference in our world, it's time to resolve to believe even when it looks ridiculous. I'm in. What about you?

> **RESOLVED:** that I will believe God is good and His Word is true even when everything in my life points against it, and that even when I fail God is still always for me and will deliver me.

2

Love When
It's Inconvenient

I once had a dog named Madam Bailey the Third. I got her when she was one year old, a big ole yellow lab. I'd never had a dog before, but I knew without a doubt that I would love this dog with all of my heart. The newspaper ad was straight up: "One-year-old well-behaved house-trained yellow lab. Will give her away. Owner ill and can't care for her anymore." If you've ever had a dog before, then you're bright enough to recognize all the red flags in that ad. Unfortunately, I wasn't that smart. I drove an hour to get her. I didn't even have a bowl for Madam Bailey's meals, but I was convinced I could have a long-term relationship with her. I'd dig up a bowl for her meals eventually.

Madam Bailey lasted exactly twenty-four hours in my home until I found her a new one.

Hold up for a second. Before you shut this book in my face, give me a second to explain. My intentions were noble and my love pure enough. What I didn't expect was the whimpering through the night, the hyperactive wagging of the tail in my tiny apartment, and the rainstorm the following morning that ended with her dragging a line of mud straight through my clean-freak domain. What I hadn't planned on was the inconvenience that love would dump into my life, and frankly, my dear, I wasn't quite ready for it.

Love is easy when it's convenient. Love is wonderful when it's reciprocated and fun and full of daisies and chocolates. But take us out of our comfort zone and throw in a wrench or two, and see how strongly we still feel about love.

Christians love to talk about love. Starting in kindergarten we sing songs about love: "Jesus loves me this I know, for the Bible tells me so." Like the rich young ruler, we know the commandments well and have convinced ourselves that we're keeping them, at least for the most part. Love God and love others. Easy peasy lemon squeezy.

But what are we really talking about when we talk about love? What do we really mean when we tell ourselves that love is all we need? If you're married, you know the kind of love that got you to the altar is not the same kind of love that's keeping you married. Somewhere between the honeymoon and the forty-third load of laundry you woke up to the fact that true love is much more than a feeling and much harder than it looks on TV. There is a predominant idea in our culture that suggests that as long as we have love for one another everything will be all right. While this idea sounds noble on paper, the reality is that no one can maintain this kind of love forever. All it takes is for someone to cut you off in traffic to understand that when we talk about love, even our best efforts at love have their limits.

Somewhere in the process of loving God and loving others we've become cynical about love. Who can blame us? Everywhere we turn we hear this four-letter word tossed around without a second thought. We've made it our mantra, our goal, our all. Love will change the world. Love will win our enemies. Love is all we need. Faith, hope, and love, but of course the greatest of these is love. Love is great—until love fails us. Despite our best intentions, all it takes is a slight inconvenience, a bad hair day, or a harsh word from someone to lose our resolve to love others well.

Love's Limits?

I'm forty-three and still single. There was a time in my life that I believed in love, but two broken engagements and an unrequited broken heart later, and you get the picture. Love is not easy and only getting harder with time. I have become an expert at building barriers around my heart. I have convinced myself that people can't be trusted. That love is too hard. That it's safer to watch from a distance. I've become selective in my love for others. I'm picky when it comes to love. I have a hunch you understand these tensions about love. You believe in God's love and agree with God's Word about love, but when it comes to practical application of that love you also cower in fear and excel at collecting self-protective devices around your heart.

I was in Jordan recently and met a Christian Iraqi refugee family who had escaped death by ISIS. I was the only member of our team who spoke Arabic, and it didn't take long for the matriarch of the family to ask for my phone number in case she ever showed up at my doorstep in need of a home. Amused, I relayed the comment to my friend, expecting her to smirk. Instead, she said, "You would have no problem doing that, right, Lina?" Ouch. Like an arrow to my heart, I felt the sting of the question. *Could I really host a refugee family with an open-ended timeline? Would I be willing to do it? Or would I throw them out the minute they spilled coffee on my carpets? Couldn't I write a check out for them to stay in a long-term apartment instead?* I was too ashamed to answer. And pragmatically speaking, writing a check might work. But is that what Jesus had in mind when He told us to love others like we would love ourselves? Was this the kind of love that Christ said would distinguish me as His disciple? Didn't Jesus understand that love has its limits, at least in the twenty-first century?

What exactly *did* God have in mind when He took on the form of man and came to earth for us? What did He really mean when He said, "Greater love has no one than this, that someone lay down his life for his friends" (John 15:13)? Did He mean it literally? It was only a few hours after making that statement that Jesus walked down the road to a hill called Calvary and gave His life on the cross for you and for me. Jesus was the very picture of God's unconditional and everlasting love for us. John understood this kind of inconvenient love. In John 3:16, the most famous verse in the Bible, John explained God's perfect love like this: "For God so loved the world, that he gave his only Son." Later in his life, John was still riveted by God's love: "In this is love, not that we have loved God but that he loved us and sent his Son to be the propitiation for our sins. Beloved, if God so loved us, we also ought to love one another" (1 John 4:10–11).

Do you want to change the world? Do you want to make a difference for God's kingdom? It's time to stop waiting for the pastor to make the first move. It's time to let go of that grudge against the in-laws. It's time to open our doors to our noisy neighbors and our hearts to our difficult co-workers. The only way to change our world is by resolving to love others when it's inconvenient and messy. The only way to stick out in a culture that is self-seeking and self-centered is to pick up a towel, lean low, and wash feet. But this kind of love is impossible without first understanding and receiving God's never-ending love for us. John summed it up like this: "We love because he first loved us" (v. 19).

We love because He first loved us.

By far the craziest thing you'll ever have to come to terms with in your life is the irrevocable, unconditional, incomprehensible, and unstoppable love of God.

Season 2

There was a time in my life when I used to think that God and I were on more level ground. I mean, I knew I was a sinner, and that Jesus had died for me, but apart from that I used to think I brought some swag to the table. And that lasted until the end of Season 1 of Lina's world. Season 2 is where things got heated up. Unexpected failures, unanswered prayers, unwanted broken dreams, unfulfilled longings, unbreakable habits, and unforeseen disasters broke down my façade of personal perfection until I had to come face-to-face with the fact that I brought absolutely nothing to God's table.

And yet He still loves me. That irrevocable, unconditional, incomprehensible, and unstoppable love of God—it's deeper than my doubts, stronger than my sin, greater than my guilt, and more than I deserve. But how quickly we lose sight of God's crazy love for us. I suppose life has a way of sucking the love out of us. We're taught that God's love can conquer anything. At first, we believe it. But after a few disappointments, we start to doubt it.

We become weighed down by our own wants.

We become afraid to give too much, worried about the ramifications of self-sacrifice, unwilling to risk it all for love.

We forget who we are in Christ.

We forget the power of God's love. The dimmer the memory of His love for us, the easier it is for us to turn instead to our favorite anesthetic for temporary gratification, and the easier it is to build walls around our hearts. Instead of pouring ourselves into the lives of others, we huddle in our corners in fear. Broken and messy, we feel like God's stepchildren. We wonder whether we've finally pushed God away with our latest failure.

So we hide. We sink into self-pity. We refuse grace. We resist God's irresistible love.

If you and I want to love others with freedom and power, we're going to have to understand God's love for us first. That's where our "swag" comes in. Our identity rooted in Christ's love is where our freedom to love others is born.

An Unbelievable Story of Love

Have you ever heard of Mephibosheth? I didn't think so. There is no better biblical example to explain the awesomeness of God's love for us than the story of King David and Mephibosheth in 2 Samuel.

David was finally the reigning king of the united kingdom of Israel. Having defeated the house of Saul, David had come through immense trials and difficulties and was finally enjoying all the fruit of his labors. God had blessed his house greatly, just like He had promised. By the time 2 Samuel 9 rolls around, we can almost feel God's favor on David's life.

One seemingly random day, David had a brilliant idea. Like a Cubs' win at Wrigley Field, David's idea seemed born out of the unexpected and shocking blue. "Is there still anyone left of the house of Saul, that I may show him kindness for Jonathan's sake?" (2 Sam. 9:1).

Say what?

While he lived, Saul had been King David's sworn enemy. He had tried to kill David on more than one occasion. No king in his right mind would voluntarily look to offer an act of kindness to the seed of his sworn and defeated enemy. Except that David had deeply tasted of God's goodness. David had received God's unconditional love. And David had made a promise to his best friend Jonathan, Saul's son, who was also dead. It didn't take long for David to find out that

Jonathan did indeed have a surviving son. His name was Mephibosheth, but he had one minor problem.

Mephibosheth was crippled.

Having suffered a fall as a young child, the grandson of Saul was broken, hurting, afraid, and one who might have been easily overlooked. Some who were watching might have even advised David to kill this heir of King Saul. But David was no ordinary man. David was a man after God's own heart. David was more than ready to be inconvenienced.

"Where is he?" he asked (v. 4).

I can only imagine what Mephibosheth must have felt when he was summoned to King David's presence. I can imagine the fear that might have paralyzed him, the feeling of nausea at the dim prospect of his future. I can imagine the shame Mephibosheth must have felt as he shuffled his way into the king's court that day. Little did Mephibosheth know what was coming. Nothing could have prepared him for the kind of love that was headed his way.

Instead of anger, David offered grace. Instead of punishment, David gave love to the crippled son of Jonathan. Instead of banishing him, David offered Mephibosheth a place at his table forever. "Do not fear, for I will show you kindness for the sake of your father Jonathan, and I will restore to you all the land of Saul your father, and you shall eat at my table always" (v. 7).

Illogical. Crazy. Radical. Unbelievable. Overwhelming. Stunning. And dumb. That's how David's actions might have been interpreted by anyone watching in the king's court that day. Even Mephibosheth was shocked. "What is your servant, that you should show regard for a dead dog such as I?" (v. 8).

David owed Mephibosheth nothing. Instead, he gave him everything. Mephibosheth saw himself as nothing more than a dead dog. Broken and filled with shame, he didn't feel he deserved anything, yet he was offered everything, including a place at the king's table forever.

The only kind of love that will change your world is a radical love that is willing to be inconvenienced enough to invite your enemy to your table night after night. This kind of love is beyond human. It's divine. It's rooted in the cross. It flows out of the Good News of the gospel of Jesus Christ, and it's God's plan and purpose for your life as His follower. This is the kind of love that will turn your world upside down and cause ripple effects beyond your wildest imagination.

So why do so many of us struggle to freely give this kind of unconditional love to others?

A Case of Mistaken Identity

We love because He first loved us. Before we can begin to love others radically, we must go back to understanding God's love for us and the power of our vertical identity. Long before that day in 2 Samuel 9, David had personally experienced God's love and goodness over and over again in his life. He knew exactly where he stood in God's eyes. Early on in his life, David had learned that God's love was not rooted in what he brought to the table but in God's very nature. External appearances would fade but God's love would never fail him. From the very beginning, when everyone had forgotten about David, God saw a ruddy-looking kid pastoring some sheep and chose him as the next king of Israel. Even the prophet Samuel was stunned. God explained things to Samuel: "Do not look on his appearance or on the height of his stature. . . . For the LORD sees not as man sees: man looks on the outward appearance, but the LORD looks on the heart" (1 Sam. 16:7).

God loves people more than anything. He loves them all: black and yellow, red and white, they are precious in His sight. It makes no difference whether you're big or small, young or old, foreign or native, male or female, gay or straight. To be honest, some days I feel more like a dead dog than God's child, unwanted and unloved. Thank God He sees past my feelings and loves me even on those days. Others might be distracted by the shuffling gait of an imperfect cripple, but God loves every hesitant step we take toward His table. You might feel broken and imperfect. God sees past your external appearance. He loves you, and He's invited you to His table forever. Too many of us fall into the trap of embracing the wrong identity about who we are. Our culture coaxes us to embrace lies about who we are. Let me give you five common mistaken identities we believe about ourselves.

1. We Are Not What We Do

When asked "Who are you?" the temptation is to tell people what you do. "I'm a doctor," we say, or "I'm a plumber." Or you might give them your marital status: divorced, single, married. If you're among Christians, your answer will reflect more familiar territory: Baptist, Methodist, small-group leader, or teacher. One of the bad habits in the ER is that we call people by their diagnosis: the wheezer, the laceration, the migraine. While HIPPA laws might have been behind the start of this practice, it is demeaning and rude. Instead, I try to remind myself to call people by their names. It's who they are. When the apostle Paul talked about his identity, he never once called himself "Bible teacher" or "writer." Instead, Paul described himself as the chief of all sinners (1 Tim. 1:15), and a "wretched man" in need of a Savior (Rom. 7:24). He described himself as "the least [worthy] of the apostles, and not fit to be called an apostle" (1 Cor. 15:9 AMP). Paul had a deep humility even though he was well aware of his credentials. He was highly educated, well known, and successful, but none of these things meant as much to him as the reality that he was beloved by God (Phil. 3:3–9). If we are Christians, our identity is not what we do but who we are in Christ. We are chosen by God, predestined for adoption, purchased by His love, saved by His grace, brought near by His blood, and made in His likeness for good works. It's imperative for us to know who we are if we are to find the freedom to love others well.

2. We Are Not Who People Say We Are

It's easy to believe your own press. You think you're cool because you're "liked," and you have an impressive number of followers and retweets. Few things are more dangerous than the comfort that other people's affirmation brings. I like to call this *horizontal favor.* Popular sells. Popular feels good. I don't know about you, but when others affirm me, it's nice. It gives me a warm and fuzzy feeling of belonging and well-being. But horizontal identity fades and people are fickle. The only way to develop horizontal impact is to understand the power of our *vertical identity.* Vertical identity is God-focused. It rests in who God says we are and what He is trying to accomplish in and through us. Are you heavily influenced by what others say about you? Do you find yourself elated by people's praise and defeated by their criticism? It's time to let go of your horizontal identity for something far better. It's time to embrace your vertical identity. You're more than who people say you are. You're exactly who God says you are—beloved!

3. We Are Not Who the Mirror Says We Are

Some consider it to be more of a female problem, but an obsession with external appearances is an equal-opportunity trap for every follower of Jesus Christ. Saul was a really good-looking guy and the people were impressed with his sex appeal. Unfortunately, he turned out to be a dud. He caved because he cared too much about what people thought of him. When God chose David, He looked past his face and straight into his heart. Do you hate what you see when you look into the mirror? Do you shudder when you stand on a scale? Have you been told you're not beautiful so many times that you've started to believe it? You were told a lie. God created you in His image. You are fearfully and wonderfully made. He sees far past your skin. He sees your heart and He loves you deeply. You might not feel worthy of love, but God found you worthy enough to send Jesus to die on the cross for you. There's nothing quite like His love.

4. We Are Not Our Past Mistakes or Our Best Performances

I grew up in a very performance-based culture. Our grades defined who we became—literally. Our career choices were made during our early high school years, and it was easy to believe that we were nothing more than our best performances and not much better than our past failures. This kind of thinking has seeped into Christian culture. You pat yourself on the back when you "do right." You think God loves you more when you're better behaved. You develop a quiet pride when you consider how much you gave last year or how many verses you've memorized. When you stop and consider it, this kind of thinking is pharisaical, nothing more. It's self-righteous and belittles the cross of Christ. Does God want you to live in obedience and to do right? Of course He does. But does His love increase in proportion to your obedience? Never!

God's perfect love frees us to know that we are more than our series of mishaps or the sum of our best choices. One of the greatest obstacles to our effectiveness in God's kingdom is our refusal to let go of the heavy weight of our past mistakes. Instead of feeling the safety of being fully known by God, we remain pummeled by the lie that God wouldn't use us if He really knew us. What is it about your past that's keeping you from your future? God already knows about your past and He still loves you. You can't out-sin God's love. You can't shock Him with your story. Of all the people God could have used to build His church, He chose a betrayer named Peter and a murderer named Paul. God will use you too, despite the weight of your past. Have you asked Him for forgiveness? Are you living in daily repentance? His grace is big enough even for you!

5. We Are Not Our Church

My birth country, Lebanon, is fascinating. Lebanese people are defined by their religious affiliation. Your name usually reflects which religious group you belong to, and when it doesn't, people are bold enough to ask you your religious preference within the first five minutes of meeting you! While this might sound shocking, it's not far removed from Western Christian culture. Soon after meeting a brother or sister in Christ, most of us want to box them in: Baptist, Lutheran, Catholic. Seeker-friendly, mega-church, Reformed, or dispensationalist. Premillenial, postmillenial, amillenial. Modern worship or old-time hymns. Satellite church or multicampus. Charismatic, prophetic, KJV, or NIV? The list is long and only continues to grow.

There was a time when I built my identity around my church. Would I make it without that particular church affiliation? Would my faith go on? Would the ministry God had called me to survive? I had stopped thinking of myself as a follower of Jesus Christ and had become identified with a specific group of people. That's a dangerous place to be. It's not the church that saves us and redeems us and transforms us. God uses the church to shape us, but it is His Spirit in us who is the catalyst for our transformation. It is Christ in us who is our hope of glory. While the church is Christ's bride, we have become too caught up with "my church"—which is typically better than "your church." We forget that the church is simply the body of believers, people who profess Christ as their Savior. We forget that it is not our doctrinal affiliations that define us but Christ's blood over us that unites us. It's time to take off our church swag and start acting like brothers and sisters in one family. It's time to love one another with the same kind of love with which Jesus loves us.

The Power of Love Unleashed

It's impossible to love others well until we know who we are in Christ. Our identity is not based on our circumstances. It rests secure in God's love. His love defines who we are. When we understand God's love for us, the power of His love can be unleashed through us, transforming our world. This kind of love is unstoppable. But first we've got to believe the truth about who we are in Christ. Now that we understand what doesn't define us, we're ready to discover who we really are in Christ.

1. We Are Alive and Well

No matter what's happening in your life or how you're feeling, if you're in Jesus you have everything you need to thrive and grow. Sometimes we just need Jesus to show us this is true. Lazarus was a friend of Jesus and had two sisters named Mary and Martha. In John 11, Lazarus got really sick one day. His sisters sent out an emergency call for Jesus, fully anticipating that He would rush to their rescue. But He didn't come right away, and by the time He finally showed up, Lazarus had died. The sisters were deeply hurt.

How could their "friend" Jesus do that to them? Didn't He care about their family? The sisters didn't understand that Christ had a bigger lesson of faith in store for them. Jesus was about to bridge the gap between what the sisters said they believed and how they lived. Jesus was about to turn their lives inside out and upside down with His healing power. But that's not where I want to focus your attention.

In John 11:43 Jesus spoke three words to Lazarus. He said, "Lazarus, come out." Now Lazarus had a choice to make. He could have stayed in the tomb, hugging his linen strips and insisting that he didn't feel alive. Or Lazarus could do the smart thing and walk out of the tomb. Fortunately, Lazarus was no dummy. We're told in verse 44 that "the man who had died came out, his hands and feet bound with linen strips, and his face wrapped with a cloth."

The moment Jesus spoke life into Lazarus, Lazarus got up and joined the land of the living. I imagine Lazarus walked around with a bit of a strut after his resurrection. Are you walking around like you're alive, or do you look more like the walking dead? Because of Christ's love for us, we are no longer trapped in a tomb. We are free forever. It's time we start acting like it.

2. We Are Forgiven and Free

Regardless of how ashamed or confined you feel right now, you are completely forgiven and free in

Christ. Most of us forget the truth of the gospel in our daily life. Remember when you first turned your life over to Jesus? You were pretty excited. But days turned into months and you slowly discovered a basic reality: you didn't stop sinning just because you got saved. And you hate your sin. You identify with Paul, who said, "I have the desire to do what is right, but not the ability to carry it out. For I do not do the good I want, but the evil I do not want is what I keep on doing" (Rom. 7:18–19). You feel like a hypocrite. You know you ought to live differently, but you can't seem to change. What used to feel like a close relationship with Christ now feels like an ever-widening chasm between your Father and you. It's time to remember who you really are in Christ. Jesus died for all of your sin: past, present, and future. He paid the price once and for all. He is not under the illusion that you're going to be perfect, and neither should you.

In Christ's days people took baths in public bathhouses. They would then put their sandals back on and walk home on the dusty roads. When they got home, they simply had to wash their dirty feet since the rest of their body was already clean. What a great picture of salvation! Though our sins have been completely cleansed in Christ at the cross, our feet continue to get dirty through the daily failings of our old sin nature. That's why we need to confess our sin daily. When we do, God promises to forgive us of all of our sin and to "cleanse us from all unrighteousness" (1 John 1:9).

If you're overwhelmed by the sin in your life, the solution is not to try harder to stop sinning. The solution is to get lower and ask for forgiveness. It's through sincere repentance that you will find it. Are you ready to humble yourself before God, who is waiting to cleanse and restore you?

3. We Are Loved and Valued

Even when you feel unworthy of it, God's love is the key upon which your joy hinges. God's love is the motivator that propels us toward greater obedience. God's love is the glue that keeps our lives together. God's love is the peace that will leave us unshaken no matter how chaotic our circumstances are. God's love is more than a slogan that gets people in the Christian door. It's more than a general concept intended to make us feel better. God's love is far more personal than a slogan. I'm talking about *you*, now. Most of us agree that God is love and that He loves the whole world. Our problem is that we don't believe God loves us, or that He even likes us. Yet God's love is personal. He cares about you and favors you. His plans are not too big to include your dreams and goals. You can drop the Cinderella act. You don't need to hide in the background anymore. God loves you. He sees you. He knows you. He's not mad at you.

One of the reasons we fail to understand God's love is that we associate His love with His gifts. We figure if God really loved us, He would give us the things we ask for. We have convinced ourselves that if God really loved us, He would make life easy for us by simply eradicating our sinful desires instead of allowing us to fail and forcing us to keep turning to Him for mercy. We figure if God really loved us He would make all of our dreams come true all of the time. We are prosperity-driven Christians at heart.

God's love has nothing to do with your circumstances. His love is steadfast and never ending. God loves you too much to cave to your every whim. He knows exactly what you need and loves you enough to accomplish His purpose for you in His time. His goal is to keep you dependent on Him through your weaknesses. You are loved. That's your true identity. It's who you are. Let this truth sink into your soul and change the way you walk and live.

4. We Are More Than Conquerors

In the middle of our toughest battles, God's power in us makes us more than conquerors. As followers of Jesus Christ, we have a job here on this earth. Jesus prayed, "Your kingdom come, your will be done, on earth as it is in heaven" (Matt. 6:10), and *you* are the means to accomplishing His prayer. Years ago, my birth country, Lebanon, was a French colony, and some positive traces of French influence are palpable in Lebanon to this day. The Lebanese speak French, dress as well as Parisians, and sit in sidewalk cafes and like French food. In fact, there was a time in the '60s when Beirut used to be called the Paris of the Middle East. If you've ever been to Paris then you might understand exactly why most Lebanese were pretty pumped about the label. Those were some good days.

Just like the French have influenced the Lebanese, we as followers of Christ ought to influence our world. We are to rub the flavor of Christ onto this world's culture, not the other way around! Does it sound impossible in a world that doesn't believe in Jesus Christ or His Word? It is impossible, except for one little detail: we are already victorious in Christ. This is a mission that we can't lose. The outcome has already been determined. Right now, as I write this chapter, Christ is seated at the right hand of God, victorious and reigning over the world. He's already defeated Satan. One day He's going to return and set up His rule here on this earth, but until then He is still the victorious One leading us on.

You might feel tired, and alone, and weak, but Christ has already given you the victory through faith. Are you telling others about the Good News of the gospel from the standpoint of victory, or are you hiding in shame and uncertainty? It is only as you see yourself victorious in Christ that you're finally free to love others without expectation or fear.

It Boils Down to This

When it comes to God's love, the reality is that we need reminders. We are healed. We are forgiven. We are loved. We are free. Now it's time we resolve to show that same kind of love toward others, no matter how steep the cost is. Like Mephibosheth, we have a choice to make: we can remain in our homes, hidden from the stares of all the other perfect-looking king's sons who act like they belong, or we can slowly shuffle our way up to the table for supper. We can believe the King and take Him up on His invitation to dinner, or we can hide.

What if love were truly possible, even for the most reprobate, irrevocably broken, unexpected cripple in the world? What if unconditional, unstoppable love were offered to you today? What if you were to freely receive it? And what if, even more radically, you were to give it to the needy in your life? Giving this kind of unconditional love requires you to be intentional and persistent. It will take you places you might not have planned on going. It might cause others to wonder about your state of mind. Most of us have no trouble loving those who are exactly like us. But true love is way more radical than that. It's the kind of love that is willing to go where others won't go and do what others won't do. It's the kind of love that doesn't define others by their religious affiliations or sexual orientation. It's a love that lasts longer than a day and is willing to be inconvenienced enough even to die for others.

It was inconvenient love that sent Jim Elliot to the Amazon jungle. It was inconvenient love that sent Hudson Taylor to China and Adoniram Judson to Burma and Amy Carmichael to India. It is inconvenient love that continues to motivate men and women today to do unthinkable acts of love: free victims of sex trafficking, forgive oppressors, serve the persecuted church, and provide water to anonymous groups of kids in remote villages in Africa.

There's nothing touchy-feely about the kind of love that sent God's own Son to die on the cross for us. This kind of love changes everything. Maybe you've been too busy to love others unconditionally. Maybe you've been too self-centered, too tired, too broken, too misunderstood, too ashamed of your past to risk loving others with the kind of love that will turn your world upside down.

Isn't it time to change? Your resolve to love others begins right now. It starts the minute you accept God's perfect love for you. But it doesn't stop there. Will you do what others won't do? Will you go where others won't go? If you long to make a difference in your world, listen carefully: you might hear the shuffling of the broken making their way to the table. Now scoot over; there's always room at the King's table for more.

RESOLVED: that I will receive God's unstoppable love for me, especially when I don't deserve it, so that I can in turn love others, especially when it's inconvenient and hard.

Obey When
It's Not Popular

This might come as a surprise, but I wasn't very popular in junior high. I wanted to be, but I had buckteeth, I spoke too fast, and my mom bought me the ugliest pair of glasses any human has ever worn. Think Mrs. Doubtfire, but without the sassy attitude. I blame all of my issues in life on this one decision of hers. How I survived those years is a mystery no one will ever solve.

Deep down we all want to be popular, or at least to fit in. The concept of "tribes" has really caught on lately. Whether it's a Facebook page, a Google circle, or a church-based community, few things feel as warm and fuzzy as the safety of acceptance. Yet God calls us to more. God calls us to obedience, and rarely does obedience feel safe.

One of my favorite sayings is this: Your walk talks and your talk talks, but your walk talks louder than your talk talks. Simply stated, obedience is walking the talk. It's moving past words to action. It's actually living out what you say you believe. In other words, obedience is a very big deal, especially for followers of Jesus. How big a deal is it? Here's how God puts it: "Whoever says 'I know him' but does not keep his commandments is a liar, and the truth is not in him" (1 John 2:4). Wow. In other words if you've ever wondered whether you're truly a Christian, take this test: "By this we know that we have come to know him, if we keep his commandments . . . whoever keeps his word, in him truly the love of God is perfected. By this we may know that we are in him" (vv. 3, 5).

In simple English, if you don't obey God, you might not be a Christian. Does that sound harsh? Those are God's words, not mine. Obedience is the ultimate test of your faith. If you say you love God but don't obey Him, you've got a problem, Roger. If you say you love God but don't do what He says, you might be lying to yourself.

What about grace? Well what about it? God is all about grace. Unfortunately too many of us use grace as a crutch to get away with disobedience. Don't get me wrong, I heartily echo the words of Paul in Romans

5, that where sin abounds grace abounds even more, but in a culture rich with its shades of gray, we're too easily tempted to cut corners and selectively obey God in a quest to remain popular.

Not once in His Word does God ever call us to be popular. He calls us to follow Jesus. He calls us to be salt in a culture that is bland and light in the darkness. He calls us to stick out, to swim upstream, to choose the narrow road. If we're looking to stand strong in the shifting sands of our culture, we must resolve to obey God even when it's not popular.

But is that even possible anymore? Is it realistic to believe we can consistently obey God's Word in today's culture? And, I mean, is it really that big a deal to live with your boyfriend before marriage? Or to watch porn if you're doing it with your husband? Or to work on Sundays if you choose to? In an era where marriage has been redefined, where morality has taken a backseat to godliness, and where independent autonomy is the norm, is it even realistic to believe that anyone can still truly live in complete obedience to God's ways?

Anything Is Possible

What would you do if, as a teenager, you were forced into political exile in Afghanistan and told to blend in to the Islamic culture or else? Daniel was a Jewish teenager among over three thousand other Jewish young men who were taken captive by their most dreaded enemy—Babylon. Babylon reflected everything that was worldly and sinful to the Jewish people. The Babylonians worshiped idols and hated the one true God. Daniel suddenly found himself not only taken captive but living among the elite in King Nebuchadnezzar's court. The king's plan was to brainwash the young Jewish minds into Babylonian culture.

The whole scheme should have been a relief to Daniel. Instead of being beaten and punished in his captivity, Daniel was being offered a reprieve. Instead of being treated like a slave, Daniel would be treated like royalty, all for the price of his loyalty over time.

Daniel could have been smart enough to see the opportunity before him. He had been selected as one of the best, the cream of the crop, and was offered a three-year free ride in the king's court. What could be better for Daniel? Just lay low and don't make any ripples. Learn what you can and enjoy the ride. Do well in school. Be cool. Who knows, you might even get a chance to share your faith with some lucky Babylonian sucker in the king's court someday . . .

"But Daniel resolved that he would not defile himself with the king's food, or with the wine that he drank" (Dan. 1:8).

Daniel just had to be different. Daniel had to stick out. He had to make a scene. While all the other Jewish young men embraced the habits of the culture, Daniel refused.

While everyone else ate meat, Daniel wanted veggies.

While everyone else drank wine, Daniel asked for juice.

While everyone else went with the flow, Daniel swam upstream.

While everyone else agreed to be a team player, Daniel opted for an individual sport.

Seriously, Daniel?

The most radical thing you can do in the world is to resolve to obey God. While everyone else might choose the easy way, the boldest thing you will do is to stick to God's principles when no one else will. In a world where even evangelicals are bending the rules for the sake of relevance, nothing will distinguish you as a follower of Jesus more than your willingness to obey God no matter how irrelevant and out of touch it seems.

Every single day is a chance for you and me to take a stand for the Lord. Every single day is a chance for us to stick out, to refuse to blend in, to be different. There were thousands of young men who were taken captive, but only Daniel chose to obey God. What gave Daniel the kind of resolve that would later change his world?

The Secret to Obedience

Obedience is not as complicated as we make it. I walk into a patient's room and recognize the familiar faces of the family I had met in the ER. We catch up. I remember that I'd treated the patient for a rash a few weeks before. I check the patient's torso, and it's clear. "How did the rash clear up so well?" I ask the family with wonder. They smile sheepishly and tell me their secret: "We did exactly what you told us, Doc."

"We did what you said." That's the secret to victorious obedience in a nutshell. Yet some people do it so much better than others. When it comes to living with a resolve to obey God, we must keep in mind three important principles.

1. We Need to Stop Looking Around at What Everyone Else Is Doing and Focus Upward on What God Has Called Us to Do

Most of us are severely obsessed with what everyone else is doing. Don't believe me? Check how many people are on Facebook these days. In a recent trip to the Middle East I was baffled to find that while some of the Syrian refugees didn't have food to eat, they had Facebook accounts on their smartphones. Our culture tells us that if it's not on Twitter it's not real. That if it's not shared it doesn't count. That if everyone likes it then it must be good. Never before has groupthink so driven our societal consensus, and never before has the pressure to conform been greater.

There are two ways to live your life: you can please God or you can please man. Paul says it like this: "For am I now seeking the approval of man, or of God?

Or am I trying to please man? If I were still trying to please man, I would not be a servant of Christ" (Gal. 1:10). You can't have it both ways. Daniel could look around and do what his buddies were doing, or he could look up and focus on what God had called him to do.

But in order to know God's call for his life, Daniel had to know God's Word. Back in the book of Leviticus, God had given the people of Israel certain laws regarding food. Meat had to be cooked a certain way and no meat offered to idols was allowed. In order to obey God's Word, Daniel had to first know it. Sadly, too many of us today have no idea what God says about anything. We have more Bibles than we know what to do with. We've got Bibles online and Bibles in every language and flavor, yet they remain untouched and unopened. Even worse, when we do open the Bible, we do it selectively and selfishly. We bend it to meet our fancy and we throw out or count as irrelevant the parts we don't care for. More often than not, we care more about what our favorite Bible teacher has tweeted than what God's Word has promised. Though the two might overlap, may God raise up a generation of followers who are more concerned with pleasing Him and knowing His Word than with fitting into the mold of whatever tribe is most popular for the day.

Only a vertical focus will free us from the horizontal pressure to conform. Only a vertical identity will free us for greater horizontal impact. You don't need other people's approval, agreement, or permission to obey God. You simply have to have the willingness to say, "Yes, Lord, I'll do what You want."

2. We Have to Become More Obsessed with God's Plans for Us Than with Our Own Agenda and Plans for Him

The Jewish men taken captive might have had an obvious agenda: to survive long enough to possibly go back home to their families. Their agenda might have been to win over the enemy with acts of love and kindness. Their agenda might have been to change the world one Babylonian friend at a time. While all of these agendas may have been noble and good, and while so many of our own dreams and goals may be noble and good, what matters is not what we dream for God but what God dreams for us. We need God dreams not human strategies. We need God plans not marketing plans. We need God goals not year-end goals. The only thing that will keep us going is the resolve to be more obsessed with God and His plans for us than our own agenda—even if our agenda happens to be a "Christian" agenda.

We have a way of making plans and Christianizing them. We call them God's plans for us, but really they are our ideas of what we want to do for God, with an "in Jesus's name" tagged onto the end. We pray self-centered and self-seeking prayers, then add the magical formula of "for Your will, and in Your name," and wait. When God doesn't step up to the plate and do what we want, we get mad at Him.

The only way to know whether our dreams for God are what He has in mind for us or not is to see how we react when those dreams fail or are delayed. My road to ministry is a perfect example of this. I came to God with so many dreams of what I wanted to do for Him. I became obsessed with my plans and agenda for Him. Since my dreams were all about Him, surely He would bless them. Since my plans were ultimately about His renown and His fame and the glory of His name, surely God would honor me with answers and abundance. Instead of the success I dreamed of, I faced many closed doors. My faith was shaken. Didn't God love me? Didn't He care about me? Why wasn't He moving on my behalf? Too often I threatened to quit. Since the outcome wasn't to my liking, I assumed that either God didn't like me or that perhaps I had misheard His call for me.

It took a long time for me to understand that God was more interested in my surrender to Him than in my plans for Him. It took a while for me to understand that God was looking for a heart to worship Him with praise even when things didn't go my way.

When you become obsessed with God's plans for your life, you truly become unstoppable. When you make God's ways for you your focus, you start living the freest life possible: a life free of anxiety. Your captivity today might not be literal but it might feel just as suffocating as Daniel's captivity by the Babylonians. You might be in captivity to the ridicule of your science professor when you confess to your faith in God. You might be in captivity to the laughter of your co-workers when they find out you're still a virgin at forty. You might be in captivity to the jeers of your family when you tell them you're giving up a six-figure income to work with orphans in Haiti. God's power in you breaks the power of other people over you, and captivity no longer has a hold on you. On the contrary, captivity becomes an adventure where you can, through your obedience to an unseen God who looks like He's abandoned you, declare that God is still good and that He is still in control of your future.

Your ability to change your world begins with your resolve to praise God in the midst of your captivity when your plans fail and your agenda blows up in your face. As you offer the fruit of thanksgiving to God, you will see Him turn your mourning into dancing. You don't have to wait for your dreams to come true to offer God the praise of your lips. Your resolve to praise God no matter what you're going through is the first step to turning your world upside down.

3. We Must Resolve to Act by Faith Today No Matter What Tomorrow Brings

Anything can happen on any given day. On any given day you might walk into the ER and find out your son has an abdominal mass that's going to end his life. On any given day you might wake up and find the enemy at your doorstep with swords in their hands and masks on their faces ready to slash your throat. As we talked about in the last chapter, life is hard and trials should be expected. Just because you're living in obedience to God doesn't mean that you're going to be spared the trials of this life. Obedience to God does not hinge on the belief that God is going to spare us the pain of living in a broken world. Lasting obedience to God is always best motivated by a response to God's love for us. It is motivated by the knowledge that though we can't guard against evil we can certainly believe God through it.

You might wonder how much faith you'll need to get through it. It's never the size of your resolve but the size of your God that makes the difference in your victory. Your resolve to obey God becomes dangerous because it is fueled by a dangerous God.

Too often we look at our circumstances and wrongly assume that God has forgotten all about us. We limit God with our unbelief. I'm constantly reminded that what kept the people of Israel from entering the Promised Land was not their immorality but their unbelief (Heb. 3:18–19).

When Daniel resolved to obey God and not eat meat, he took a huge risk. He didn't know that his decision would bring him success. When he approached the chief eunuch with his request, the eunuch said,

"I fear my lord the king, who assigned your food and your drink; for why should he see that you were in worse condition than the youths who are of your own age? So you would endanger my head with the king" (Dan. 1:10). The eunuch was afraid. But Daniel was undaunted. When you resolve to obey God, God will give you the courage you need to stand strong despite opposition. Daniel could have resigned himself to apathetic conformity simply because he ran into a roadblock, but he did not. Daniel strove to obey God, and God made a way for him to do so. He asked again. "Put me to the test," he offered. "God will come through for me" (see vv. 12–14).

Three years later, Daniel stood before King Nebuchadnezzar and was found to be ten times better than all the other guys. You and I have no idea what tomorrow will bring. For some it might bring pain and more suffering and perhaps even persecution. But for some it will bring favor and success here on this earth and maybe even the chance to be promoted in the land of your captivity. What God does promise, for all who resolve to obey Him, is that come rain or shine, His name will be glorified forever, and herein is enduring joy and lasting satisfaction.

It's not *that* we resolve but *what* we resolve that matters. Every year millions of people make New Year's resolutions and break them before the end of January.

The reason is that this kind of resolve is focused more on our own desires and needs and whatever fad is most popular that year. God-sized resolve is far more than a low-carb diet or a treadmill. It's based on obedience to His Word and trust that His character will come through for us even when everyone around us might think we're being just a little bit too radical. When we resolve to obey God, we're declaring to a watching world that God matters most, that this God we've given our lives to will come through for us, and that He is good and in control no matter how bad the circumstances in our lives may seem.

This kind of faith moves mountains and transforms hearts. If the world is underwhelmed by Christians, it's largely because we bend at the merest inconvenience. We opt for popularity instead of pain. We choose worldly pleasures and temporary comforts at the cost of all we say we believe. Personal appetites and people pleasing may give us some sense of immediate gratification, but living without resolve will result in long-term disappointment and a negligible impact. The time to resolve to act boldly is when the stakes are high and we're uncertain of the future. The time to act obediently is when it doesn't make sense and we feel forgotten.

You might feel like you're living in the land of captivity. God is with you even there. Though Daniel did see some tremendous fruit for his obedience, God never did deliver him from the Babylonians. Yet he remained faithful and never lost his impact. Daniel understood that freedom had nothing to do with his location and everything to do with his King. The apostle Paul could say the same thing. Even when he was in prison, the world's system couldn't touch him. He saw himself first and foremost as a prisoner of Christ. No wonder he was used by God to change the world.

What would our world look like if every follower of Jesus Christ resolved to obey God, especially when it's not popular? How would our world be different if every one of us resolved to live by faith, walking the talk and not just talking the talk, and refused to give in to our personal appetites?

You might think the life of obedience is a lonely life. It is, but God always provides what we need when we need it. For Daniel, God's provision came in the form of three young men named Shadrach, Meshach, and Abednego. They saw Daniel's resolve and followed. We learn a very important lesson about obedience: when we're willing to stand alone for God others will follow.

Shadrach, Meshach, and Abednego saw Daniel's resolve to obey God and took the challenge. They didn't want to watch from the sidelines. In that moment a community was born in the land of their captivity. You don't need a lot of people to change the world. You don't need thousands of followers and bestselling books and stadiums full of people. All you need is the living Word of God and His faithful presence. When you resolve to obey God, you will turn your world upside down. God will always come through for you. He does it in His way and in His timing. He gives us the strength when we feel weak and the tenacity when we want to quit.

You might have resolved to obey God in the past and failed. That's where God's grace comes in. Today is a chance for you to resolve afresh. What's keeping you from making up your mind to obey God? What's keeping you from starting again? God is faithful. Ask Moses after forty years in the wilderness, or Abraham after twenty-five years of waiting for a son, or Sarah at ninety when she was pushing Isaac out, or Joseph after a decade as a slave, or David once he was seated on the throne: God always comes through for His people. And He's going to come through for you!

RESOLVED: that I will obey God even if no one else is doing it and even when the outcome is unclear, knowing that God always honors radical obedience to His ways.

Yield When It's My Right

I hate yielding. There's a yield sign that comes up on my way to work right after I take the exit off the highway. As I get closer to the sign, I glance to the left and barely stop long enough to blink. I figure I've got it. I can drive faster than the other guy. One of those days I'm going to crash and burn. Until then, I revel in my ability to rise above the crowd and win.

The Western mind in particular chafes at the idea of yielding. As early as elementary school we're taught to be strong, to pull ourselves up by our bootstraps, to strive for greater independence. The minute we turn eighteen we're expected to move out, to make it on our own. Our world becomes a man-eat-man, woman-pushes-woman free-for-all. May the strongest survive.

Against this frenetic mindset of self-sufficient, self-reliant, self-governing autonomy stands the way of Christ. Fundamentally, the call to discipleship is a call to yield. It's a call to self-denial. It's a call to say "you go first" even when it might be our right to go first.

- "If anyone would come after me, let him deny himself and take up his cross daily and follow me" (Luke 9:23).
- "I have been crucified with Christ. It is no longer I who live, but Christ who lives in me" (Gal. 2:20).
- "You are not your own, for you were bought with a price. So glorify God in your body" (1 Cor. 6:19–20).
- "So therefore, any one of you who does not renounce all that he has cannot be my disciple" (Luke 14:33).

You get the picture. You cannot choose your own ways and faithfully follow God. The call to discipleship is an all-in total takeover of who we are. It's a willingness to say "Yes, Lord" even when we feel like saying no. It's not a self-improvement program. It's a total transformation. It's not a face-lift. It's a heart transplant. It's not a minor procedure. It's a

general-anesthesia-going-to-be-in-the-OR-until-
we're-through-with-this-procedure journey of learning how to yield to God in every way imaginable.

No wonder Jesus warned His hearers to seriously
count the cost before following Him.

> Which of you, desiring to build a tower, does not first
> sit down and count the cost, whether he has enough
> to complete it? Otherwise, when he has laid a foun-
> dation and is not able to finish, all who see it begin
> to mock him, saying, "This man began to build and
> was not able to finish." Or what king, going out to
> encounter another king in war, will not sit down first
> and deliberate whether he is able with ten thousand
> to meet him who comes against him with twenty
> thousand? (Luke 14:28–31)

Most people couldn't handle it. When they heard
the sales pitch of Jesus to follow Him, many of His
disciples turned back and no longer followed Him
(see John 6:66).

What about you? Are you still in or is this too much
for you to handle? This is serious business and only
the yielded need apply. Thankfully, yielding to God
is not a solo sport. Your teammates are God's never-
ending grace and the presence and power of His Holy
Spirit in you. There is nothing you cannot do when
the Holy Spirit is your guide. Have you ever heard
of the "I Am Second" movement? It's a modern-day
Christian website where people are videotaped giving

their stories of following Jesus and always end it with this statement: "I am second." There's Bethany Hamilton, the surfer whose arm was bitten off by a shark; Scott Hamilton, the Olympic gold medal skater who despite cancer is still yielding to God; and Lecrae, the Christian billboard rapper who survived abuse and still gives God the glory for his success.

We applaud these people and their stories. We amen them. We nod our heads in agreement. But when push comes to shove and God actually tests our resolve, many of us can't hack it. We walk away or at the very least choose to live pathetic lives of disillusionment in God. No wonder Jesus warned us: "No one who puts his hand to the plow and looks back is fit for the kingdom of God" (Luke 9:62).

Yield in the Details

The thing about yielding is that it's easy to do when it involves something you don't care about that much. Once a year my sister forces her kids to clean their closets. They're asked to put aside stuff they no longer need and give it to charity. You won't catch them arguing when they yield their least favorite jackets and unloved toys.

I was recently at Target with those same nephews. They each had five dollars to spend in pursuit of their latest obsession: LEGO minifigures. Each of these figures is about 2 cm in height and barely visible to the naked eye. Each comes with a tiny tool like a sword or pizza box. My nephews easily have about a hundred of these LEGO figures and they love each of them with a love that surpasses all other loves. On that particular day, Micah, the twelve-year-old, made his choice but his little brother Ben decided to save his money. It took all of two minutes after leaving Target for Ben to regret his decision and beg Micah to let him touch his new LEGO figure. If you have preteen boys who love their toys, I don't need to tell you how miserable the ride home was.

Yielding is not easy when you love the thing you're being asked to yield. When it comes to our walk with the Lord, every day is a chance for us to yield. What will we choose? God or our silly little toys? God or that one thing we think we can't live without? Sadly, too many followers of Jesus are regularly opting for their peanut-sized LEGO figures instead of the brilliance of God Almighty. No wonder the world is underwhelmed by our representation of God.

If you're serious about changing your world for Christ, and if you're serious about living what you say you believe, then it's time to resolve to yield to God in every detail of your life—in the big things and the small. God is just as interested in your yielding to Him in your eating choices and television-watching habits as He is in your choice of a career and spouse. See, yielding is about your heart. Either your heart is the Lord's or it's not. And typically, before He asks us to yield in big things, God will train us to yield in the small things.

But It's My Right of Way

No story illustrates the concept of yielding better than the story of Abraham. When Abraham left his hometown of Haran, he took with him a few other people, including his wife Sarah and his nephew Lot. You might have heard of Lot. He's the guy who lived in Sodom. But before Sodom, Lot was just a young nephew who was mentored by his uncle Abraham. If you know anything about Middle Eastern culture, then you might pick up on some of the family dynamics that would have been at play here. Abraham was the patriarch, the mentor, the father figure, and the one in charge of Lot. As such, he demanded the respect of the people he was leading simply because of his position. Add to that the fact that Abraham was greatly favored by God and that he was a very rich man, and you'll understand that Abraham was a man of great caliber, one who typically would have had first choice in where he lived and how he lived.

In other words, Abraham was a big deal in the eyes of everyone around him, and Lot was more or less a beneficiary of all the good things that had happened to Abraham. Any normal nephew would likely have idolized the ground that Uncle Abe walked on, and I have a feeling Lot looked up to Abraham tremendously.

As time went by both Abraham and Lot became richer, to the point where the land couldn't handle them both. It was time to split up. Instead of forcing his way on Lot, Abraham made him this offer: "Let there be no strife between you and me, and between your herdsmen and my herdsmen, for we are kinsmen. Is not the whole land before you? Separate yourself from me. If you take the left hand, then I will go to the right, or if you take the right hand, then I will go to the left" (Gen. 13:8–9).

I am second. You before me. That's what Abraham was offering his nephew Lot, and it was radical in every way because of his age and position and role in Lot's life. Now if you're from the Middle East, then you would be aware of some of the social dances that are traditional and expected. You would understand that no never really means no, and that an invitation to action is never accepted on first request. So if you heard Abraham make this offer, your knee-jerk reaction would be to answer, "No, no, Uncle Abe. You go first. You choose, then I'll choose." Every oxygen-breathing Middle Easterner would know that. What would then ensue is a dance lasting a few steps where I would offer you the first choice, then you would offer me the first choice, and so on and so forth. It's exhausting and sort of amusing.

Technically speaking, Lot would eventually have to cave because of his age and position. That's what would be expected. In this case, though, things went down a little bit differently. There was no such social dance. Lot simply "lifted up his eyes and saw that the Jordan Valley was well watered everywhere like the garden of the LORD, like the land of Egypt, in the direction of Zoar. . . . So Lot chose for himself all the Jordan Valley, and Lot journeyed east" (vv. 10–11).

Yikes. Lot looked. Lot saw. Lot chose, and Lot went. And it all went downhill for Lot from that point on. There isn't one positive story about Lot after this verse.

Are you tracking with me? We're talking about yielding, and when it comes to yielding what we choose will always affect the outcome of our lives. Abraham yielded to Lot even though it was his right to go first. Lot refused to yield. The ramifications of each decision were huge. For Abraham, God showed up and honored him. After Lot left, the Lord said to Abraham:

> Lift up your eyes and look from the place where you are, northward and southward and eastward and westward, for all the land that you see I will give to you and to your offspring forever. I will make your offspring as the dust of the earth, so that if one can count the dust of the earth, your offspring also can be counted. Arise, walk through the length and the breadth of the land, for I will give it to you. (vv. 14–17)

God isn't interested in how well watered the land we choose is. He cares more about the condition of our hearts than the condition of our lands. He can take the driest land and turn it into a garden. He makes a way in the sea and a path through the storm. All He asks is that we yield to Him by putting all of our trust in Him. Our yielding will always produce fruit because God's promises never fail.

> Blessed is the man who trusts in the LORD,
>   whose trust is the LORD.
> He is like a tree planted by water,
>   that sends out its roots by the stream,
> and does not fear when heat comes,
>   for its leaves remain green,
> and is not anxious in the year of drought
>   for it does not cease to bear fruit. (Jer. 17:7–8)

Yielding is powerful, and it will change your world. Refusing to yield will destroy you. Lot took matters into his own hands. He moved closer and closer to sin and eventually ended up in disaster. His home was destroyed, his wife became a pillar of salt, and his daughters drugged him in order to sleep with him. He became the grandfather of his own kids. Lot's story is sick, and it's sad, and it's heartbreaking—and it all started when he chose his way instead of yielding to Abraham.

Learning to Trust God's Best

Ultimately, yielding is about trust. It's about faith. It's about believing that God is who He says He is and that

God will do what He promises He will do. Yielding moves from the driver's seat to the passenger seat and refuses to be a backseat driver. Yielding is powerful because it elevates God to His rightful place of worship. Yielding to God is a declaration that *I am not God, but I trust God with what's best for me.*

If it sounds impossible, then you're on the right track. But God has not left us on our own in this. He has given us three provisions for the battle to surrender.

1. We Need the Help of the Holy Spirit

Do you ever wonder why God didn't create a magic bullet to help us in our times of need? Technically speaking, He did.

The Holy Spirit is the magic bullet who makes it all possible. He's the One Christ promised to give us after His departure from this world (John 16:7). He's the Spirit of God who came to dwell in our hearts the moment we turned to Christ for salvation (1 Cor. 12:13). He's the third member of the Trinity, eternal and holy. He's the One who draws people to the gospel and the One who equips us with strength to accomplish God's purposes for us. He convicts us of sin (John 16:8–11; 1 Thess. 1:5). He intercedes for us when we pray (Rom. 8:26). He is our seal of salvation (Eph. 1:13). He's our hope and freedom and joy and peace, and He's our sanctifier (Gal. 5:22–23). He is our power over sin (Rom. 8:2). Most importantly, He's our help in time of need, the One who gives us the ability to yield when it feels impossible. If you're trying to yield without the Holy Spirit, no wonder it's not working so well. Whether it's for a more consistent prayer life or in finally getting victory over that recurrent sinful habit, ask Him to help you where you're failing.

2. We Need God's Word

God's Word is food for our soul. In Psalm 119 we're told that God's Word revives our soul, makes wise the simple, rejoices the heart, enlightens the eyes, and endures forever. God's Word is light for our path. It's our sword in our battles. It contains everything we need. It is more than sufficient to give us strength and guidance. God's Word is alive and active and is a discerner of the thoughts and intents of our hearts.

We need God's Word if we want to yield well. I mentioned that yielding is about trusting God. It's about hoping for things unseen. When we don't see the way, the only thing we can hang on to is God's Word. When our feelings betray our fears, only God's Word will give us the strength and the stability to endure through the storm. If you're not growing in the knowledge of God's Word, you're probably not going to have what it takes to endure through the trials in your life. Most Christians would agree that it's important to grow in God's Word, but how? I was twenty years old and starting medical school when I heard that it takes twenty-one days to form a habit.

I figured that might work in developing a consistent Bible reading pattern, which might in turn help me through med school. It did. Over the years, though, I have found that simply reading God's Word is just the beginning point. The point of reading God's Word is to get to know the God of the Word. The more you meditate on what He says, the deeper that Word will penetrate your life and change you. As you memorize His Word, God will use it to remind you and encourage you and comfort you when you need it. And if you're not sure how to pray, many authors have described the simplicity and effectiveness of praying God's Word back to Him. Try starting in the psalms.

If you're starting to feel overwhelmed by all this, don't be. Remember that Rome wasn't built in a day. God tells us in Isaiah 28:10 that we do this "precept upon precept, precept upon precept, line upon line, line upon line, here a little, there a little." It's a daily process of growth and learning.

3. We Need Unending Grace

Have you been there before? Have you tried yielding and failed? That's what grace is for. God's grace is new every morning. You don't need to fret over your past failures. You don't need to hide from your uncertain future. All you need is the unending grace of God that will pick you up when you make wrong choices. There is no sin so dark that God cannot forgive it. There is no failure so recurrent that God cannot deliver you from it. There is no bondage so tight that God cannot destroy it and set you free from it. I'm speaking from personal experience. I am writing this book today because of God's grace. I've failed more often than I like to remember, but I'm still here and God is still using me. He is that faithful and good. He'll do the same for you!

Everyday Yielding

One of the scourges in my life is talking to customer service reps on the phone. Every conversation is a battle to yield. Will it be their way or my way? Since I'm the customer, I figure it should always be my way. The warranty should last longer, the benefits should be better, and the delivery should arrive faster than it typically does. I have a strong sense of entitlement. I suppose I tell myself that I'm highly educated, highly respected, highly paid, and highly driven. It doesn't take much for me to believe my own press. But all it takes is one conversation with a customer service rep to remind me that I'm not great at yielding.

What about you? Are you getting stronger with time? Is your faith in God growing? You can gauge how strong you are by your willingness to yield. I know I'm failing in yielding when I:

- lose my patience too quickly.
- demand my rights too forcefully.

- refuse to wait like everyone else does.
- spend more time talking than listening.
- choose to argue instead of saying thanks.
- feel more joy in getting my way than in showing kindness.
- waste too much time trying to win my way through the argument too readily.
- overlook the opportunity to win a soul for the opportunity to win an argument.

Every day is a chance for us to practice yielding. Every day God is training us to hold the things of this world loosely and hang on with dear life to His presence and His Word. Every day is a training arena to help us get stronger in faith. We don't have to win every argument—even if we know the facts and we are right about them. We don't have to prove our point to the world just because we know we're right. God certainly does want us to speak the truth and intelligently fight for the gospel, but when it becomes too personal and stops being about God we simply must learn to lovingly yield.

The Biggest Tests

When we resolve to yield ourselves in small things, we'll find ourselves ready to yield in the big things too.

For Abraham, the big test came from left field. He'd finally had his long-awaited promised son, Isaac. Life felt good. God had proven Himself faithful. And then one day, "God tested Abraham and said to him, 'Abraham! . . . Take your son, your only son Isaac, whom you love, and go to the land of Moriah, and offer him there as a burnt offering on one of the mountains of which I shall tell you'" (Gen 22:1–2).

Talk about yielding in the biggest thing! The closer you walk with the Lord the steeper the test will be. The more you walk intimately with God and see His faithfulness, the more you will be asked to trust everything into His care. The Christian life doesn't get easier with time. Rather, we become more dependent with time. God is constantly in the business of making us stronger. Stronger in reliance on Him and stronger in faith. Stronger in hope and stronger in endurance. No, it doesn't get easier with time, but the same God who was faithful in Genesis 13 is the God who is faithful in Genesis 22.

When Isaac asked his father about the lamb for the offering, Abraham said, "God will provide for himself the lamb for a burnt offering, my son" (v. 8).

God is always able to provide everything we need. You don't have to know how. You simply have to yield. You're asked to yield when it looks ridiculous. You're asked to yield where others might not. You're asked to yield where it hurts the most, and where you desire the most.

It was hard for me to end one engagement, let alone two. But I gladly did it for the chance to serve God with all of my heart. I saw my singleness and broken engagements as fuel for serving God with more zeal and passion. What took me by surprise was God's demand that I offer Him the only thing I had left: my dream of serving Him in ministry. It seemed cruel to me that God would take my lesser dream of marriage and then ask for my deepest dream of serving Him in ministry, yet His demand was unmistakable. *Lina, give Me your ministry.*

God will provide for Himself a lamb. Our part is to walk up the hill and tie the sacrifice to the altar. Ours is to say, "Yes, Lord, I'll do what You want." Then out of the woods, or caught in the thicket, we will see the perfect lamb for the offering that God has provided.

Abraham passed the most difficult test of his life when he walked up that hill with Isaac at his side and a few scraps of wood on his back to build an altar for God. "By faith Abraham, when he was tested, offered up Isaac. . . . He considered that God was able even to raise him from the dead, from which, figuratively speaking, he did receive him back" (Heb. 11:17, 19). The more difficult the act of surrender, the purer the offering will be. I'm not sure what makes us think that surrender is going to be easy. It's not. Giving to God what matters most to us is heart wrenching. It's devastating. It's painful. And it's worth every drop of blood we shed for that offering. Because when we finally raise the knife to offer the sacrifice, we're declaring to a watching world that God is better. That God is great. That He is good and faithful. And that He will provide exactly what we need.

Jesus understands the cost of surrender more than anyone else on this earth. Kneeling in Gethsemane just hours before His crucifixion, He prayed so hard He sweat drops of blood, and said, "Father, if you are willing, remove this cup from me. Nevertheless, not my will, but yours be done" (Luke 22:42). Unlike with Abraham, there was no lamb in the thicket to save Jesus from the hour. Jesus *was* that perfect Lamb of God whose blood was shed so that we would be free.

What's so amazing about Jesus is that three days later He rose from the dead. He overcame sin and death and now sits at the right hand of God making intercession for us. That same Jesus is the One who is asking us to yield everything to Him. In return, He's promised to be faithful. He's promised to be with us. He's promised to give us His unstoppable love forever.

What is it that God is asking you to yield to Him today? Is it a desire for marriage or for kids? Is it a relationship, a dream, a business, a ministry, or your lifestyle? Whatever it is that He's asking, God is able to do more than you can imagine in restoring it one-thousand-fold. What is keeping you from yielding to Him in big things and in small? Some of the most common reasons for not yielding to God include:

Our fears. *What if God doesn't come through for me?*
Our pride. *Doesn't God want me to be happy?*
Other people. *What will they think of me if I do it?*
Our addictions to pleasures. *What if I'm miserable?*
Our material possessions. *Can I afford to lose it?*
Our frenetic pace. *Can I fit one more thing into my day?*

This is a battle that begins in the mind. Paul says, "But I am afraid that as the serpent deceived Eve by his cunning, your thoughts will be led astray from a sincere and pure devotion to Christ" (2 Cor. 11:3). Satan is a master deceiver. He knows exactly how to distract our attention from the only One who will give us deep and lasting joy: Jesus. He plays on our fears and insecurities and fools us into thinking that we will only be happy if God will finally do exactly what we want.

The only way to stay deeply in love with Christ is to, over and over again in the course of the day, tell Him you love Him and show it by choosing Him over everything else in your life.

This is what it means to be a Christian, a fully surrendered follower of Jesus. It's a radical all-in total takeover of who you are with no turning back. Anything remotely close to this will demand your unwavering resolve and the belief that God is the only treasure worth selling everything for.

RESOLVED: that I will daily give up my rights and say yes to Jesus in big things and small, even when I feel like saying no, confident that surrender is the pathway to joy.

Speak Up When
It's Easier Not To

I remember exactly where I was the day I resolved to speak up for God without apology. I've already mentioned that I wasn't very popular in junior high. Things changed as I got older, and by the time I reached medical school my cool factor was on the rise. I knew I was reaching new ground a few weeks into my first year of med school when Shelby and John asked me to join them for a study group.

You have to understand that Shelby and John were "it." They embodied everything I had wanted to be in junior high and high school. Now that I'd finally graduated from my Christian college and was starting a new adventure, I permitted myself to do a happy dance over the prospect of being part of the "it" crowd.

If you know much about study groups, then you know that the first thirty minutes are wasted. People catch up. They gossip and kill time until the urge finally settles upon them to, in fact, study. I was a little bit nervous walking into that study group. I didn't want any of my old dork factor to show up. I had agonized over what to wear and had finally settled on a casual but stylish study outfit. I was greeted with smiles and laughter and my heart swelled within me. If only my old junior high self could see me now.

And then it happened. A name came up, a kid in our class who I thought was cool. It was Shelby who said it first: "He's so weird. He's a born again. Those folks are all crazy."

Say what? Born again. Weird. Crazy. In case you missed it, that "those folks" included me. By that time in my life I was an all-out Christian. I had thrown my stick in the campfire and written my favorite verse in the flyleaf of my Bible. Jesus was my Lord. I loved Jesus with all of my heart.

Yet in that moment, I froze. I said absolutely nothing. Crickets.

The moment passed. We finished studying. And the minute I got back to the crushing silence of my apartment I made this resolve: from that day forward I would speak up for God no matter what.

I never joined that study group again. I also finally understood what Peter must have felt when he heard the rooster crow. I understood what it meant when he went out and wept bitterly. I had turned my back on the One who had given me everything. I had betrayed the Savior I loved. I had chosen my popularity over the name of Jesus. I had chosen the safety of acceptance over the privilege of standing up for the truth. But never again would that happen to me.

You and I have a responsibility. We know the way, the truth, and the life. We have been given grace upon grace. We have been loved and accepted and forgiven and set free. Anyone who has come face-to-face with God's goodness and embraced it knows that we have a duty—even more, a privilege—to share this truth with others. It's easier to stay silent. It's easier to aim for acceptance. It's easier to hide in the shadows hoping that someone else, somewhere else, will be the one to speak the truth.

We're living in a culture of hyper-tolerance. Everyone wants to fit in. We're told we have the freedom to do anything as long as we don't impose our opinions on others. Many of us have interpreted that freedom as the need to stay politely silent. We're afraid. What will happen if they find out what we really believe about marriage being a covenant between one man and one woman for life? How will they treat us when they figure out we really believe what the Bible teaches about the homosexual lifestyle? Will they think we're too drastic, too judgmental, too harsh? What if they don't agree with us? Instead of walking in obedience to our Lord, we've chosen to keep our beliefs private. We have forgotten that the impact of our silence can be deadly for many. In choosing the safety of silence, we have condemned many to a life apart from God's goodness and grace.

Suppose a patient came to my ER with a deadly infection that could be cured with an antibiotic. And suppose the family was known to be opposed to medication. And suppose out of respect for the family, I chose not to tell them about the medication that could be lifesaving. If the patient died and it became known that I had withheld knowledge of the prescription, I would be sued for malpractice. No judge in this land would deem me kind for holding back what could have saved the patient's life. No jury in the world would commend me for "respecting the family's wishes." Our responsibility is to speak up with the truth. We must do it lovingly and kindly. What people do with the truth is their responsibility, but ours is to speak up no matter the cost.

If we really believe what we say we believe, then we have a duty as followers of Jesus Christ to speak the truth when it's easier not to. Anything less than that is stark disbelief.

But What If It Costs Too Much?

The price for speaking the truth can be high, sometimes too high. I mentioned King Nebuchadnezzar earlier and it's time to revisit him. Nebuchadnezzar was the king of Babylon and he was pretty full of himself, so much so that he decided to build a gold statue of himself and force everyone to bow before it. All the leaders around Nebuchadnezzar agreed to the harebrained plan and signed the petition. There was one caveat to it: "And whoever does not fall down and worship shall immediately be cast into a burning fiery furnace" (Dan. 3:6).

Do you want to know how the people in Babylon responded? You bet. When the people heard the sound of the music, they did exactly as they were instructed: they "fell down and worshiped the golden image that King Nebuchadnezzar had set up" (v. 7).

Everything would have been A-OK except for one thing. Some people, three to be exact, refused. Their names were Shadrach, Meshach, and Abednego. Remember them? They had a choice to make. They could bow down to the king's idol like everyone else did, or they could speak up with the truth, even when it certainly was easier not to. The Chaldeans were local leaders who hated Shadrach, Meshach, and Abednego. They were jealous of them. They hated the fact that these foreigners had become leaders and rulers in their land and they wanted them out. So much so

that the Chaldeans approached King Nebuchadnezzar and pointed out the fact that Shadrach, Meshach,
and Abednego had refused to bow to the king's statue.

King Nebuchadnezzar went into a furious rage and
commanded that the three men be brought to him.
"Is it true . . . that you do not serve my gods or worship the golden image that I have set up?" he asked (v.
14). He then gave them one last chance to bow down
and an ultimatum: "If you do not worship, you shall
immediately be cast into a burning fiery furnace. *And
who is the god who will deliver you out of my hands?*" (v.
15, emphasis added).

Challenge served. King Nebu versus Almighty God.
Game on. Shadrach, Meshach, and Abednego are at
a crossroads. It's a crossroads many of us are familiar
with.

It's the silent pause after Shelby and John viciously
attack all born agains. It's the moment after the servant
girl accuses Peter of being a friend of Jesus. It's the
moment you've probably faced at a family reunion or a
dinner party. It's the moment every Christian business
owner dreads when he or she is asked their stance on
marriage. It's the moment the Christian surgical resi-
dent must decide what to do about abortion training.
It's the moment everyone at work is laughing about
the newest R-rated movie and you're tempted to laugh
along. It's the moment you finally think you've found
the one, the man you've been waiting for, but he wants
to go all the way. Do you give him what he wants and

count on God's grace to cover it all, or do you stand up and speak the truth, risking so much?

Nebuchadnezzar cries, "Who is the god who will deliver you out of my hands?" Is God trustworthy when everything seems to point against Him? Is His Word true? Will He come through? Why doesn't He just stand up for Himself? Does He really want me to be the one to tell the world how to live their lives? Can't I just bow my knees to the king and in my heart still hold on to the Lord? What about love? Isn't love a better strategy for winning people than speaking the harsh truth to them?

Our hope is that we can slip on by without making a scene, and we long to justify our actions. Yet day after day many are being killed for the sake of the cross all over the world. In China Christians meet in secret to worship the King of kings. Do they really have to have a church service? Can't they just worship God in private? In Iran followers of Jesus are held captive and persecuted for refusing to deny the Savior. Can't they say what they're being asked to say in order to be set free and later— perhaps much more quietly—tell the world what they really believe? In Iraq Christians are kicked out of their homes by the Islamic State for refusing to bow their knees to Mohammed. Is it worth the struggle? Is it worth the fight? Doesn't it cost too much to speak up when it's easier not to?

For Shadrach, Meshach, and Abednego, the choice was clear. "O Nebuchadnezzar, we have no need to answer you in this matter. If this be so, our God whom we serve is able to deliver us from the burning fiery furnace, and he will deliver us out of your hand, O king. *But if not, be it known to you, O king, that we will not serve your gods or worship the golden image that you have set up*" (vv. 16–18, emphasis added).

It's almost the exact thing that Peter said to his accusers when commanded not to speak about Jesus anymore. Peter, who had already tasted the agony of betrayal, now answers boldly and clearly: "Whether it is right in the sight of God to listen to you rather than to God, you must judge, *for we cannot but speak of what we have seen and heard*" (Acts 4:19–20, emphasis added).

We can't help but speak! We've been set free. We've been redeemed. We've been protected and helped and saved and given new life. We can't help but speak of what God has done for us. No matter what it will cost us, we will open our mouths and speak the truth! If you're wondering how you'll have the strength to carry out the resolve to speak up for Christ when it's easier not to, it helps to remember these four principles.

1. The Resolve to Speak Up Comes from Really Knowing What We Believe

No one shows up for a test without studying—unless you intend to fail. In order to pass the test with flying colors, first you've got to be enrolled in the class, and then you've got to know the material. Unless you really do believe that Jesus is the way, the truth, and the life, you're probably going to have a hard time standing up for Him. Unless you really do believe that His Word is the highest authority in your life, you're going to have a hard time speaking it out. We're living in a day where people—even followers of Jesus Christ—have become Bible skeptics. We own Bibles but are too busy to read them. We rely more on our feelings and less on God's Word in living our lives. We read blog posts and tweets instead of the Old and New Testaments. We wait with eager anticipation for our favorite author's next bestseller instead of hungering for God's Word. No wonder we fail in the test to speak up for God. We don't even know what God wants anymore. Today is the day to resolve to open God's Word and learn to rightly handle it (2 Tim. 2:15). When the time comes, He'll give you the words to say.

2. The Resolve to Speak Up Is Based on Who God Is, Not What He Will Do for Us

Modern-day Christianity seeks out God for what He'll do for us. We look for God to give us life, riches, and happiness. We talk about God's favor and forget that legions of men and women before us saw God's favor on their lives as they were tortured and beaten and ridiculed and killed for the sake of the gospel. Somehow, we think we're exempt. The writer of Hebrews described men and women of faith this way: "They went about in skins of sheep and goats, destitute, afflicted, mistreated—*of whom the world was not worthy*—wandering about in deserts and mountains, and in dens and caves of the earth" (Heb. 11:37–38, emphasis added). These men and women understood that when it comes to a life of faith that stands up for the truth, it's not about what God can do for us. It's about who God is.

Do you feel more favored by God when He gives you what you want? Do you believe His love is truer when your prayers are being answered the way you want them to be? You might be confused about who God is. And who is God? He's the One who never changes. He's the same yesterday, today, and forever. He's the Almighty Savior, the Creator and Sustainer of this world. He's the loving Messiah, the King of kings. He's the only One worthy of our worship. He's our unconditional Advocate, Comforter, and Provider of all we need. He's the One who paid the price for our eternal lives. He's worthy of our praise. Peter understood it. The three brothers understood it. And if you've come into a saving knowledge of Jesus, then you get it too.

3. The Resolve to Speak Up Is Easier in a Group but Necessary Individually

There's power in accountability and in doing life in community. The longer I live the more I understand that who I surround myself with will directly impact my destiny. "Do not be deceived: 'Bad company ruins good morals'" (1 Cor. 15:33). At times we'll have to stand alone, but strength comes in numbers. The wisest man in the world wrote that, "though a man might prevail against one who is alone, two will withstand him—a threefold cord is not quickly broken" (Eccles. 4:12). Your friends can make or break you. If you're a follower of Jesus Christ and can't point to a couple of God-fearing, God-loving, God-pursuing Christians helping you through life, chances are you're going to cave at the crossroads of your test to speak up for Jesus.

Even though there's great power in community, the resolve to follow Jesus and the resolve to speak up for Him must be made individually. There's no way around it. Your parents can't decide to take a stand for you. Your spouse can't speak up for you. Your pastor or small group leader can't make this decision for you. Only you can resolve to know God and His Word and to spend your life in His undivided pursuit.

4. The Resolve to Speak Up Is Tested When the Stakes Are High

When King Nebuchadnezzar heard the brothers' resolve, he "was filled with fury, and the expression of his face was changed. . . . He ordered the furnace heated seven times more than it was usually heated" (Dan. 3:19). He turned up the heat so high that the men who threw Shadrach, Meshach, and Abednego in the fire were themselves burned up by the flames. The stakes were very high. The cost was very steep. And the brothers fell bound into that burning fiery furnace.

Those who oppose Christ naively believe that binding our wrists with their shackles can somehow bind God's Word. They are wrong. Over the last few months I have watched the imprisonment in Iran of a young Iranian American Christian pastor, a former Muslim who converted to Christianity in 2000. In 2012, he was detained in Iran and sentenced to eight years in prison on charges of undermining the Iranian government by creating a network of Christian house churches and attempting to sway Iranian youth away from Islam. Today he is still in captivity waiting for his freedom. To the watching world his fate seems sealed. His future looks grim. All efforts at getting this American citizen his freedom seem futile. Yet every time I read something about this young man I'm pumped just a little more to stand up for the kingdom of God. His willingness to pay the price for following Jesus presses me to get stronger and remain undaunted by the enemy.

I met a twenty-eight-year-old woman when I was in Lebanon. She had given her life to Jesus over a year ago and was filled with joy. I asked her story. How was her Muslim family responding? "My parents don't talk to me anymore," she said. "And my husband left me and I only see my two kids on Sundays." Don't be fooled, the stakes are high when you walk in obedience. The price might seem unimaginable. You might be rejected by your closest friends and hated by your family. You might suffer pain and you might even die. But if you're a follower of Jesus Christ then you understand that you've already died and you're alive forever. You've been crucified with Christ. You now live, but you no longer live for yourself. You now "live by faith in the Son of God, who loved [you] and gave himself for [you]" (Gal. 2:20).

A Huge Ray of Sunshine

The truth is that speaking up for Jesus isn't always as hard as we think it will be. The light of God's love will inevitably shine through us as we live our lives for God's glory. I've learned to come out of the Christian closet very early in my friendships and relationships. That way there are no surprises. When people know what we stand for, it often spares us the need to say too much. It's our actions people are watching. While things might not always work out the way we think they will, as followers of Jesus Christ we always have strength in the name of the Lord. And in the end, things will eventually work out for our good.

King Nebuchadnezzar thought he'd won the war, but he hadn't even won the round. After throwing the brothers into the fiery furnace, he "was astonished and rose up in haste. He declared to his counselors, 'Did we not cast three men bound into the fire?' They answered and said to the king, 'True, O king.' He answered and said, 'But I see four men unbound walking in the midst of the fire, and they are not hurt; and the

appearance of the fourth is like a son of the gods'"
(Dan. 3:24–26).

When God's presence is with you, the fire has no
power over you. The same God who will lead you into
the fire is the God who will walk into the fire with
you. The same God who promises that "when you
walk through fire you shall not be burned, and the
flame shall not consume you" (Isa. 43:2) is the God
who will keep that promise. He did it quite literally for
Shadrach, Meshach, and Abednego when they were
thrown deep into the furnace.

The power of the Christian is that we don't have to
fear the fiery furnace. God has overcome every fiery
furnace we will ever face. If we're looking to impact
our world, it will happen when we learn to trust God
unflinchingly and completely. The power of our testimony is loudest when we're in the fiery furnace. The
presence of God is most visible when we're walking
through the fire. King Nebuchadnezzar saw it. He was
so overwhelmed by the outcome that he blessed the
name of the Lord. He wrote a new decree: "Any people,
nation, or language that speaks anything against the
God of Shadrach, Meshach, and Abednego shall be
torn limb from limb, and their houses laid in ruins,
for there is no other god who is able to rescue in this
way" (Dan. 3:29).

God's arms will always catch you when it feels like
you're falling. You might not see the outcome on the
front end of the test. You'll have to walk by faith, not

by sight. But every test you take to speak up when it's easier not to is a chance to live what you say you believe. It's a chance to lift up the name of Jesus and declare that He is indeed worthy of your trust. The strength of your resolve has less to do with the outcome of the matter and everything to do with the One you're committed to.

Do you believe that God is good no matter what? Do you believe that God is able to deliver you no matter what? The story might not always end the way that you want it to, but when you put God first in your life, He will always come through for you in ways you can't begin to imagine.

Many men and women in this life have stepped out in faith to speak the truth. Some were delivered, but many were not. Jim Elliot was killed by the very men he was trying to reach for Christ. James, one of the disciples, was killed in prison by Herod while Peter was miraculously delivered. Even John the Baptist, one of the greatest disciples who ever lived, had his head chopped off while Jesus went about performing miracles.

The goal of the Christian life has never been temporary earthly comfort. This earth is not our home. Christ Himself said, "For whoever would save his life will lose it, but whoever loses his life for my sake will save it. For what does it profit a man if he gains the whole world and loses or forfeits himself?" (Luke 9:24–25).

You must decide for yourself. What are you living for? What do you want more than anything? The breadth of your impact will be determined by the depth of your resolve to follow Jesus and speak up when it's easier not to. Trusting God might not always yield visible results and significant promotion and the praise of people. But your resolve to obey will always be met with God's faithful presence.

Stephen was a man who could have remained quiet. He wasn't even an apostle. He was simply a man who followed Jesus and His ways. When put to the test he refused to remain quiet. His last words on this earth as he was being stoned to death were, "Lord, do not hold this sin against them" (Acts 7:60). To the watching world, Stephen's life might have seemed like a waste. To the jeering crowd, Stephen looked defeated. To the angry mob, Stephen got what he deserved. No one, after all, dare stand up against popular culture and win.

But one man was watching. He was the one who had ordered Stephen's murder. He heard every word that Stephen spoke out. His name was Saul. You might know him better as the apostle Paul.

Your resolve to speak up might bring you ridicule and shame. But what if you too had a watching Paul in the shadows whose very life might be radically transformed by your resolve to speak the truth at any cost? What if your resolve could change the world of just one person? Wouldn't it be worth it all?

RESOLVED: that I will boldly and unashamedly speak up for the gospel, admitting my allegiance to Jesus Christ and His Word, knowing it might cost me my life but certain that God's presence is always with me even through the fire.

Give When
I Barely Have Enough

Safety isn't just a word. It's a feeling. And when it comes to money, for the longest time in my life I defined my safety by my financial condition. If I could grow my financial cushion enough, then I'd finally be safe. It shouldn't have come as a surprise to me, then, that for over twenty years of my life every time I built up that cushion, God compelled me to give it away. Let me be honest with you: at first I didn't like it. I wanted to be safe more than anything. I wanted to know that I would be okay on a rainy day. I wanted to breathe more easily and dream bigger dreams. In other words, I was in bondage to money. My bank account had a clutch hold on my life and wasn't letting go.

While in Lebanon I met with a man who's done more for God's kingdom than anyone I know. He's built churches and trained leaders. At almost eighty years old he still travels into danger zones, where the Islamic Jihad is killing Christians, simply to encourage the church and give hope to the needy. I told him that I wanted to minister to Arabs, and especially Muslims. I told him I was desperate to get involved in ministry. His eyes got big and he smiled, "I know just the place for you. I just got back from Kurdistan," he told me. "And they need a pediatrician. They can pay fifty dollars a day. You could move there right now!" I didn't have to do the math. My heart had stopped at fifty dollars a day. I could barely pay one of my bills at fifty dollars a day. Didn't this pastor understand my worth? In that very same breath, I realized I had a money problem.

We are living in stressful days. No matter how hard we work, it never seems to add up: our bills are too high, our needs are too many, and our ability to keep up is too small. Even when we do our best to cut our expenses and work even harder, money is never enough. Admit it. Weren't you tempted to skip this chapter? Who even has energy to talk about giving when we barely have enough? Even if we were to find our own personal cash cow, most of us would use the extra funds to pay off our debts and maybe finally take that family vacation we've dreamed about.

As long as we're enslaved to our wallets, we will have little impact on our culture. The world is not impressed with people who claim that God is more than enough, that Jesus is all we need, and that we're living for eternity when our day-to-day lifestyles reflect an unusual attachment to the things of this world. The world is underwhelmed by Christians who claim that God is able to provide for our needs while all the while we clutch our stuff in anxiety and wonder where we'll come up with enough cash to afford our newest gadgets.

Few things will stick out in our culture like the resolve to pursue a lifestyle of giving generously and sacrificially when it's unexpected, unnecessary, or uncomfortable. Nothing will point to the worth of the Savior more than our willingness to open our hands and give all that we have for the sake of something bigger than we are, more eternal than we'll ever be, and far more important than our temporary needs.

The Amazing Power of Giving

There's something extremely powerful about giving when you barely have enough. It actually feels great—I mean it *literally* feels great. Have you experienced it before? I've found that the harder it is for me to part with something, and the more I love it, the greater the blessing I feel when I give it. I know I'm not alone in this. There once was a boy and his lunch. Never in his lifetime could he have expected that his lunch of a few crackers and a couple of fish would make it into history forever. Never in her lifetime could his mother have imagined that her meal that day would become a symbol of so much that is good in this life.

The crowd was hungry. The disciples were tired and begged Jesus to call it a day. But Jesus had a plan that was about to blow everyone away, and said, "They need not go away; you give them something to eat" (Matt. 14:16). Don't you love it when Jesus asks you to do what seems impossible? No amount of food that day could have fed that crowd, and the disciples knew it. Was this a joke? Still, one of the disciples must have made an effort, because of all the people in the crowd, one boy stepped up with his brown paper bag. Five loaves and two fish were all he had but also all he gave when he barely had enough (John 6:9).

Do you ever wonder what could happen if you'd give your all to Jesus when you barely have enough? The need will always be so much bigger than what we have to offer. It's easy to get overwhelmed. But God isn't concerned with the size of the need. He's not dependent on the size of our offering. What God wants is simply all that we have.

"Bring them here to me," Jesus said (Matt. 14:18). *Give Me what you've got.*

God wants only what we have. It may seem little or it may be big, but all God asks for is only what we have. Whatever is in your hand is what He's asking you to give. He asks not because He needs it but because He knows that's where the miracle begins. Jesus ordered the crowd to sit down, said a blessing, then proceeded to feed every single person in the crowd. With every broken piece of bread another person was fed. Everyone ate. Everyone left satisfied. Not one was overlooked. And it all started when one boy gave all that he had— just five little loaves and a couple pieces of smelly fish.

You will never know the power of God to provide for you until you give Him all you have. Are you tempted to argue and show me that it's stupid to give everything to God, and that God doesn't want us to be unwise? You're missing the point, and you might just be in bigger financial bondage than you suspect.

God tells us a whole lot of things about money. Here's a sampling of His view on money:

- "Love your enemies, and do good, and lend, expecting nothing in return, and your reward will be great." (Luke 6:35)
- "Give and it will be given to you. Good measure, pressed down, shaken together, running over, will be put into your lap. For with the measure you use it will be measured back to you." (v. 38)
- "When you give to the needy, sound no trumpet before you, as the hypocrites do. . . . But when you

give to the needy, do not let your left hand know what your right hand is doing." (Matt. 6:2–3)

- "Do not lay up for yourselves treasures on earth, where moth and rust destroy and where thieves break in and steal, but lay up for yourselves treasures in heaven, where neither moth nor rust destroys and where thieves do not break in and steal. For where your treasure is, there your heart will be also." (vv. 19–21)

- "You cannot serve God and money." (v. 24)

- "The love of money is a root of all kinds of evils." (1 Tim. 6:10)

- "But those who desire to be rich fall into temptation, into a snare, into many senseless and harmful desires that plunge people into ruin and destruction." (v. 9)

- "Do not withhold good from those to whom it is due, when it is in your power to do it." (Prov. 3:27)

- "Whoever has two tunics is to share with him who has none, and whoever has food is to do likewise." (Luke 3:11)

- "Give to everyone who begs from you, and from one who takes away your goods do not demand them back." (6:30)

Do you get the point? Money matters to God, but what God cares even more about is the condition of our hearts: Do we trust Him?

Most of us live in financial bondage. We have way too much debt. We spend way too much time worrying about our bills and what we will do in case of an emergency. We put our trust in our dollars and almost never trust God with our security until we are in full-blown crisis mode. When it comes to money, God is fairly clear. First, He wants us to put all of our trust in Him instead of in our checking accounts. And second, God wants us to make wise and God-honoring choices with the funds He's given us.

When it comes to money, at least in the Western world, we've screwed it up. We've got pastors living in million-dollar mansions and Christians killing themselves to make just a little bit more. We watch while the rest of the world is dying of hunger and drinking filthy water from dirty rivers. We're unmoved by the state of our own brothers and sisters in Christ, and when we are just a little bit moved, our giving is so marginal we might as well skip it. No wonder the world is confused by us.

On the one hand we sing, "This world is not my home; I'm just passing through," while on the other hand we're trying hard to claim our piece of this world. Paul didn't have trouble understanding the truth. He had given up everything to follow Jesus, and from the dank prison floor he wrote these words: "But our citizenship is in heaven, and from it we await a Savior, the Lord Jesus Christ" (Phil. 3:20). The writer of Hebrews explained it this way: "For here we have no lasting city, but we are seeking the city which is to come" (Heb. 13:14 AMP). And we're told this as the testimony of those who've walked ahead of us in faith:

> These all died in faith, not having received the things promised, but having seen them and greeted them from afar, and having acknowledged that they were strangers and exiles on the earth. For people who speak thus make it clear that they are seeking a homeland. If they had been thinking of that land from which they had gone out, they would have had opportunity to return. But as it is, they desire a better country, that is, a heavenly one. (11:13–16)

Are you living with your heavenly home in mind? Or is your heart planted here on this earth?

How Can I Diagnose the State of My Giving?

If you're still with me, chances are you really do want to make a difference in your world. You want to walk the talk. You long to make an impact for Christ. You're tired of the status quo, and you're hungry for a breakthrough. Good. Let's figure out how to identify the state of our giving. Here are four diagnostic tests to help us assess how we're doing in giving.

1. The Test of Sacrifice

It's called the widow's mite because it wasn't much bigger than a mite. While everyone else walked up to the offering box with heavy coins and large sums of money, the poor widow shuffled up with nothing but two small coins worth a penny. Jesus saw the whole thing and commended the widow. "This poor widow has put in more than all those who are contributing to the offering box. For they all contributed out of their abundance, but she out of her poverty has put in everything she had, all she had to live on" (Mark 12:43–44).

Are you giving until it hurts? If you're not, it might not be enough. My goal isn't to tell you how much to give, but I do know the pattern in Scripture. Over and over again people left everything to follow Jesus, and over and over again God provided for them. When you give Him what you have, He will do what you can't. Stop worrying about how you're going to live and resolve to follow the widow's example. Give sacrificially. Give until it hurts. Give wherever you see a need. And you'll see. The world will sit up and pay attention.

2. The Test of Ridicule

In John 12 it's Mary, Lazarus's sister, who's ridiculed for giving too much. Overwhelmed with gratitude for all Christ had done for her and for whom she recognized Him to be, Mary took a pound of perfume and washed Jesus's feet with it, using her hair to wipe them. Her offering cost her so much. Judas, who later betrayed Jesus for thirty pieces of silver, laughed at her, and asked, "Why was this ointment not sold for three hundred denarii and given to the poor?" (v. 5). He didn't care about the poor, but he did care about money.

Most of the people who will ridicule our giving have not deeply tasted the grace of the Lord Jesus Christ. They have no understanding of the meaning of the abundant life. Paul commanded us to set our minds on heavenly things, not on earthly things (Col. 3:2). The mind that is fixed on heavenly things will do crazy and radical stuff. Take my friend Jackie as an example. Most people take it easy after retirement. They travel and read. Not Jackie. At sixty-five she saw a need and acted on it. She poured her own savings into buying an apartment to use as a safe house for abused women—in West Beirut, of all places! Today, seven years later, Jackie gets calls in the middle of the night to counsel victims of abuse. She told me how recently members of Hezbollah drove around the city and on the very street where the house is located, in search of a woman who had sought shelter there. Jackie was on her knees with the women in the house, praying, while God gave them the protection they needed.

Jackie continues to ridiculously pour funds and energy and time into helping a handful of women out of their life of bondage. Some have turned to Jesus while others have not, but all have tasted the love of the Savior at least for a moment. I'm amazed by what God has done through Jackie as she has given Him rightful ownership of all that she has. Some may mock Jackie for her efforts and consider her unwise and without concern for her own safety, but those who have experienced the joy and grace of dangerous giving are inspired by her example to do even more for the sake of the gospel.

3. The Test of Joy

I'm a very disciplined and principled person, and I believe God's promises. As such, I have made it a point to continue tithing even during seasons of financial strain in my life. But for the sake of full disclosure I have to admit that there is a test I've failed more often than I like. It's the test of cheerful giving. "Each one must give as he has decided in his heart, not reluctantly or under compulsion, for God loves a cheerful giver" (2 Cor. 9:7).

Sadly many of us give because we believe in the principle of sowing and reaping. While the principle is a good and biblical one—God does promise to bless us when we cheerfully give to Him (2 Cor. 9:6–11)—we have the knack of molding it into our own version of a Christian benefits plan. Because we want God to bless us, we give, but we do so reluctantly or under compulsion. I've been guilty of giving because I want God to reap bountifully in my life. Haven't you too?

We figure that if we give God His due, He'll give us our due. The truth is that we will never out-give God. And this kind of giving is not true worship. Cheerful giving says much more about our God than simply giving out of duty. Cheerful giving is an act of trust that shouts out that our God is able to do far more than we can ask or imagine simply because He's good. And that even if He doesn't provide an immediate, tangible return, He's still worthy of our praise. Cheerful giving is an act of worship that elevates God to His rightful place and highlights His true character.

Dennis is a friend of mine. About twenty years ago he had just started following Jesus and was trying to figure out new life in Christ. One Sunday his pastor taught the congregation this law of sowing and reaping. Dennis decided to take up the challenge of giving. That first year, Dennis expected God to honor his giving. Instead, his business did worse than any other year to date. Dennis went to his pastor with resentful questions. His pastor felt bad but held on to God's Word. "Dennis," he said, "I'm not sure why your business has done worse now that you've decided to honor God with your finances, but I know what God's Word says." Dennis resolved to keep on giving. That following year, and every year since that time, God has blessed Dennis above and beyond what he could imagine. Giving is no longer a hardship for Dennis. It is his complete joy. It's his new way of living. Dennis retired a few years ago, and today he volunteers as an art teacher to children simply because he's looking for even more ways to give! God is always faithful. You take the test of giving cheerfully and you'll find out for yourself just like Dennis did.

4. The Test of Need

The prophet Elijah went to Zarephath to stay in a widow's house. These were days of famine, yet the first thing Elijah did upon arriving was to ask the widow for water and for bread. Overwhelmed by her own need, the widow sheepishly answered, "As the LORD your God lives, I have nothing baked, only a handful of flour in a jar and a little oil in a jug" (1 Kings 17:12). Elijah was undeterred. "Do not fear; go and do as you have said. But first make me a little cake of it and bring it to me, and afterward make something for yourself and your son" (v. 13). Elijah's request may have sounded arrogant, but it wasn't. It was a test of faith. Would the widow trust God to meet her need when that need became desperate? Would she step out in obedience even when she barely had enough? God more than met her need. Her act of faith was greatly rewarded. For the entire season of famine the widow and her family had more than enough for all of their needs. The jar of flour was never spent and the jug of oil was never empty.

You will never put God to the test and find Him lacking. In fact, God challenges us to put Him to the test in Malachi 3. When we give to Him sacrificially and cheerfully and consistently and worshipfully, He will open the windows of heaven and pour His blessing on us.

I'm not a pastor. I'm not going to end this section with a call for an offering. Your money makes no difference to me. But here's what I do know: money does not satisfy. The more you make, the more you will need. I should know. I never seem to make enough. We're living in days where people need hope. People are looking for answers that satisfy and for light in the darkness. What if God were to raise up a generation less concerned with personal comfort and more concerned with personal sacrifice?

Until we resolve to give even when we barely have enough, we will have no influence in a world that is motivated and driven by greed and material possessions. We must resolve to be different. *We are different.* We are followers of the King. He owns the cattle on a thousand hills. He controls our world in every detail of its functioning. We don't have to be afraid of natural disasters. We don't have to worry about the future. We can rest knowing that He will guide our ways.

Excuses We Make for Not Giving

So why don't we give? If we say we believe God is our provider and that He wants us to give, why then don't we do it more freely? Why, in a crowd of five thousand adults, did only one kid offer his lunch to meet the need at hand? Why is it so hard to apply what we believe about giving? I believe there are four common excuses we use for not giving.

1. I Don't Trust the Church

Too many Christians have become cynical about the church. In the era of mega-churches and celebrity pastors, it's not hard to become jaded when it comes to giving to the church. When your pastor shows up in a Jag and minutes later is preaching about the importance of helping the poor, it's easy to roll your eyes and overlook the offering plate when it's passed.

The thing about giving to God is that you don't have to trust the church. You simply have to trust the Lord. Don't get me wrong. God gave you a brain and the ability to make decisions, but if you don't trust your church enough to give to it, it might be time to find a new church. No matter where you go to church, though, God holds people accountable individually for how we steward what He's given us. None of what we have is ours to begin with. It's all His. When you think about it, we've all been given a whole lot of grace for acting like it's ours.

2. I'll Do It When I'm Rich

"Tomorrow, tomorrow, I love you tomorrow, you're always a day away." When it comes to giving, few excuses are as powerful as the excuse that you'll give when you make just a little bit more. But you're never going to feel like you have enough. If you don't give when you're poor, you won't give when you're rich. Giving is a matter of the heart. It's a reflection of who and what you worship. Stop waiting for the mood to strike. It never will. Start walking by faith and give sacrificially no matter how much your net income is. You're never too young to learn these principles. My nephews are ten and twelve. They're taught the same biblical principles that you and I know from God's Word. When they make as little as one dollar, they have a saying: "We give some, we save some, and we spend some."

They get it. The question is, do you?

3. I Don't Believe in the Principle of Tithing

Christians are funny. We spiritualize everything. I can't tell you how often I've heard people argue that they don't give because they believe that tithing is an Old Testament principle that no longer applies to us as followers of Jesus.

Here's what I do know: the early church was a giving church. They gave so much that no one in the church had unmet needs. They pooled their resources together and they gave. In fact, here are the exact words from Acts: "And all who believed were together and had all things in common. And they were selling their possessions and belongings and distributing the proceeds to all, as any had needs" (2:44–45). Want to know the result of this radical kind of living? "And the Lord added to their number day by day those who were being saved" (v. 47).

The church grew. Revival ensued. The culture was turned upside down. If you're thirsty to see your world change, you might want to start living like the early church did. Look for need and meet it. Stop living so safely. Give. It's an investment that keeps on giving.

I know what you're thinking. You're wondering if I've gone off the deep end. I have not. I'm not asking you to sell your house and live on the street. I'm not even telling you to throw away your clothes or give away all your savings. I'm just suggesting that we each ought to stop long enough to listen to God's voice when it comes to how we're spending the resources He's given us to steward. We might be surprised what He tells us. We might find out that He's far more interested in you helping other people than in buying another home. You might even end up making some serious changes in your lifestyle.

4. I'll Trust God to Provide for the Needy

If God can do anything, why can't *He* just provide for the needy? Isn't that God's job? Why doesn't He just do the miracle? The best part about God's kingdom is that He uses us, people like you and me, to expand His kingdom. He uses our gifts. He uses our resources. He uses our lives to make a difference in others'. We get to be a part of the process. I told you earlier that every time my financial safety net grew, God compelled me to give a big chunk of it away. At first I was frustrated with God. I even tried to ignore Him. But in every occurrence, His leading was clear. And here's what I learned: in all my years of living, I have never once regretted giving God His due. I've never been in need. Not even once. There have been times where I've felt some financial strain, but it's the kind of strain that has driven me to my knees in prayer. As I've prayed, God has provided—over and over again. And my story is not unique.

George Mueller is a favorite in my family. My nephews are obsessed with him. Many have attempted to minimize his faith. "The myth of George Mueller," some have written. I respectfully disagree with his critics. George Mueller was a man who believed God. He never asked for donations. He simply laid the need out and prayed. Over and over again God provided, not just for his needs but for every child he cared for in his orphanage. I think about the number of lives impacted by George Mueller. We will spend eternity hearing the gorgeous details of faithful followers of Jesus who gave faithfully expecting nothing in return.

If you're looking to change your world, resolve to give when you barely have enough. Resolve to believe that God not only can but will provide for your need. God will take the little that you give Him and turn it into much. He's faithful and He's good. He'll never let you down. Just ask the little boy with the brown paper bag. He'll tell you that it's when you let go of what's in your hand that you'll see the miracle happen.

RESOLVED: that I will never hold back from giving cheerfully and willingly even when I barely have enough, knowing that God is always faithful and will always provide for all of my needs.

7

Be in Community When I'd Rather Be Alone

I'm a typical single. I live in the paradox of complaining about being alone but I'm also an expert at avoiding community. I recognize my need for people but run from small-group gatherings. I want others to reach out to me but feel burdened by any insinuation that I'm to reach out to others. I am quick to come up with a list of reasons why I can't commit to the few invitations that come my way but also quick to complain when everyone stops inviting me over.

If you connect with any of these isolation techniques, then you might not like this chapter. When it comes to living by resolve, no decision will impact your world more than the decision to live in community. Yet most of us run at the mention of the word.

I'm writing this chapter less than a week after returning from my birth country of Lebanon. In the ten days I was there, I was invited to more homes than in the last year in the United States. I was fed more meals and called more times than I could keep count of.

We in the Western world live our lives differently. Our culture is facing an endemic of independence and isolationism like never before. With singleness rates as high as 53 percent of the population, we have become accustomed to living on our own. The effects are not only detrimental but counter to God's plan for us. It will take some serious resolve to choose God's way of community when we've adjusted to being alone.

Created for Relationship

If you're not sure that God values community, you can go all the way to the beginning for some proof. In Genesis 1, God reveals Himself as a God in community: "Let us make man in our image, after our likeness" (Gen. 1:26). Who was He referring to? The "Us" of God continues to be a mystery but is a reference to the Trinity: God the Father, God the Son, and God the Holy Spirit. This kind of community is unique to the God of the Bible. This is a God who loves relationship. In Genesis 2, when God created Adam, He assessed all that He had created and said, "It is not good that the man should be alone; I will make him a helper fit for him" (v. 18). And so Eve was created.

God loves people. He loves relationship. He loves community. No wonder He created the church and called it the body, the bride of Christ. He came to earth in the form of a human named Jesus in order to make a way for us to be in community with Him. We are only afforded one right in our lifetime, and it is the right to be called children of God (John 1:12). The minute we place our faith in Jesus and receive Him into our hearts, we're adopted in God's family. Now that's relationship in its highest form!

Yet despite God's love for relationship, and despite God's plan to put us in relationship with Himself and with other people through His church, we run and hide from relationships like nobody's business. We often choose to isolate ourselves, even when we're in a crowd.

Walk into any public forum and you'll catch myriads of people with their heads down, staring at a palm-sized screen, lost in another world. Alone. Walk into any church today and you'll find the same thing. We avoid looking into people's eyes lest they demand more from us. We place well-built walls around our lives and dare anyone to cross those invisible barriers. No wonder our impact is so limited. People are afraid to approach us. They can read our body language. They can tell we don't have time, interest, or energy for them.

I suppose, when you think about it, it's easier to be alone. It's safer to isolate. But ultimately it's unwise and it will ruin us to continue down the path of isolationism. We were made for more. We were created for fellowship, and I'm not talking about apple pie and coleslaw in a church basement. I'm talking about real fellowship, real community, and real people.

Why Do We Avoid Community?

Before we can begin to talk about what real community is, it's important to zone in on why we choose to isolate ourselves instead of living in community. The best way to understand it is to study the poster woman for isolationism. We meet her in John 4. She doesn't even have a name. Even today we still just call her "the Samaritan woman." She's been there. She's done that. And frankly, she's tired of it all. So she's set her own path in this world. She's doing life on her terms, and she's all alone at the well.

One thing's for sure, the Samaritan woman wasn't looking for an encounter with the divine on that particular day. She wasn't looking for community. And she certainly wasn't looking for conversation. If she had been, she might have chosen a different time to go to the well. Instead she chose the noon hour to fill her jar of water. It was the hottest hour of the day. I suppose if you're trying to avoid running into anyone, that's exactly when you'd go to the well. In the case of the Samaritan woman, that was precisely her goal. Why was the Samaritan woman looking to be alone? There are typically four reasons we choose to isolate ourselves from others.

1. We Are Painfully Aware of Our Past

The Samaritan woman had a past. She'd had a rough go of life. She'd been married five times and was presently living with a man who was not her husband. You might miss the severity of her issues in today's culture. I know a woman today whose mother has been married nine times, so in our Western context we might think that multiple marriages and a live-in boyfriend aren't biggies. But back then, and even today in Middle Eastern culture, the Samaritan woman was carrying some pretty heavy sinful baggage. She knew exactly what and who she was. So she avoided others. She hid. She chose to isolate herself from the accusing looks of others.

The opposite of isolation is intimacy. It's hard to be intimate with others, and to open your life to them, when you're weighed down by the burden of your own sinful and wrong choices. It's easier to hide. I've

145

been there before. The last place I want to be when I'm choosing to sin is in the presence of others who might find out exactly who I really am. Have you ever been there before? It's a heavy weight to carry, and it might be time to let it go.

2. Others Are Painfully Aware of Our Past

The only thing worse than knowing who we are is the notion that "they" know who we are. If you live in a small town, you've probably felt this kind of shame. You hear the whispers. You catch the stares. For the Samaritan woman, the weight of the shame was so heavy that she took great care to avoid even running into the villagers at the well. She chose the hottest hour of the day to cover her shame. They say sticks and stones will break our bones but words will never hurt us. Yeah, right. We've all experienced the unbearable shame of other people's words. It's far more painful than any wound a knife can wield.

The last thing the Samaritan woman expected that day at the well was the very presence of Jesus. He sought her out when no one else would. He found her even when she wasn't looking for answers. I wonder what went through the Samaritan woman's mind on that day when she showed up to the well and found a man waiting. I wonder if she looked down and avoided His gaze. I wonder if she tried to turn around and leave.

Shame has a way of keeping us from living. What are you ashamed of? Is it your past? Is it your present?

146

Is it the mistakes of your husband or children? Is it an illness you can't hide? While other people might try to shame you, Christ in His love comes near you. He knows who you are and He loves you. That's where community starts.

3. We Are Ashamed of Our Past

I hate feeling like I'm on the outside looking in. It doesn't take much for me to fall into the trap of self-condemnation. *I'm such a fool. How did I let it happen to me—again?*

I'm useless, worthless, friendless. No wonder they don't want to be around me. I'll never amount to anything. I'm good for nothing.

If you've ever felt like this then you understand the power of self-condemnation. If you're a follower of Jesus Christ there is no room for lies in your life. Aren't you tired of punishing yourself out of living life to the fullest? Many of us isolate ourselves as a form of punishment for our mistakes and insecurities. While God hates our sin, He loves each of us deeply. He loves us so deeply that Jesus left His friends in the middle of the day, and despite being hungry and exhausted He made His way to the least likely place in the least likely village to speak with the least likely person in the world: a Samaritan and a woman no less. The Samaritans were considered a people who were "less than" the Jews. They were avoided at all cost. And women . . . well, women didn't even deserve to

147

speak in public places. Yet Jesus found the Samaritan woman with the messed-up past simply because He loved her. He loves you too. No matter what you've done or where you've been, God loves you and thinks you're worth it. "See what an incredible quality of love the Father has shown to us, that we would [be permitted to] be named and called and counted the children of God" (1 John 3:1 AMP). That's amazing grace.

4. We Punish Ourselves for Our Past

I've written much about self-pity in my life because I've fallen prey to it so often. Like an unexpected pothole, self-pity trips me up and keeps me stuck when I least expect it. I'm too single, too scarred, too ugly, too talkative, and too abrasive to be included in the throng. Woe is me. I sink deep into the pit of self-pity with little hope for deliverance. Elisabeth Elliot has said of self-pity that "It is a death that has no resurrection, a sinkhole from which no rescuing hand can drag you because you have chosen to sink." The idea that we deserve what we get is void of the truth of God's love. *We deserve what we get until Jesus walks in.* We deserve what we get until Christ paid the price. We deserve what we get until Jesus sets us free. Do you avoid relationship with others because of the sense that you don't deserve the grace of community? It's called grace because it's undeserved, and it's yours in Christ today.

What is it that's keeping you from life in community? Are you hiding in sin? Are you sinking in self-pity? Are you punishing yourself for your own mistakes? Or are you simply ashamed? If you're not careful, you'll find yourself alone at noon in the heat of the day. Your wounds will fester. Your impact will be blunted. Pretty soon you'll find yourself stuck in a pattern of defeat that will rob you of joy. It will rob you of your freedom. It will rob you of any sort of power in your life.

Dealing with Selective Authenticity

When it comes to fixing our problem of loneliness and isolationism, too many of us attempt to fix our problems with our own solutions. It's time to talk about selective vulnerability and partial authenticity.

I've discovered a new "four-letter word." It's the word *vulnerable*. To be vulnerable is to be susceptible to being wounded or hurt. It's opening yourself up to attack. It's setting yourself up for possible rejection and pain. That doesn't sound like something I want to sign up for, do you? Yet when it comes to finding true intimacy, it's impossible to accomplish without vulnerability.

This longing for intimacy that we have is God-given. Whether you're single or married, male or female, God created you for intimacy. The problem most of us have is that we've tried the path of vulnerability and failed. We opened ourselves up, and the very thing we dreaded happened. We were hurt. And if we're honest with each other, we don't ever want to feel that kind of pain again. The fear of future hurt simply outweighs our willingness to risk being vulnerable again. Our past hurts keep us from future intimacy. So we settle for selective authenticity without being completely vulnerable. We choose the pieces of ourselves to share with each other. We make ourselves look better than we really feel. And we wake up and find ourselves still alone, still longing to be loved and accepted beyond our wildest imagination.

You know what I'm talking about. You show up to small group and convince yourself that you're living in community. You tell them exactly what you want them to hear. You're truthful—to a point. You're authentic—as long as it stays within the realm of safety. You're selectively vulnerable, and you know little of true community.

You leave your community just as alone as when you entered and wonder why the Christian life feels so trite. You self-medicate with more sin. You self-protect with more denial and hiding. You give up. But what you don't expect is Jesus, sitting by the side of the well, waiting to break through your longing for intimacy.

In Psalm 139 the psalmist, King David, stumbles upon true intimacy and is forever changed. "O LORD, you have searched me and known me! You know when

I sit down and when I rise up; you discern my thoughts from afar. . . . If I ascend to heaven, you are there! If I make my bed in Sheol, you are there!" (vv. 1–2, 8).

David understood that though he was more sinful and flawed than he ever dared believe, he was also more loved and accepted than he ever dared hope, to borrow a turn of phrase from Tim Keller. His response was to make himself even more vulnerable to the love of God. He ends the psalm with a plea: "Search me, O God, and know my heart!" (v. 23). There is safety in the perfect love of God, and that love finds its pinnacle at the cross. The cross is the place where you and I are totally seen—all of our sin, our imperfections, our failures, and our needs lie bare before the eyes of the Savior, who still chose to love us enough to die for us. If you're looking for the freest form of living, it starts with a four-letter word called *love*. Only Jesus can heal our hurts. Only He can give us the intimacy we long for.

There was a time in my life that I clung to sin. I was hurting and lonely, and God hadn't answered my prayers the way I wanted Him to. To be completely honest, I was disappointed with God. I had assumed that if I played my part, then He'd deliver His. It didn't have to be exactly what I had in mind, but I expected Him to land in the general vicinity. Instead, it seemed like I was on the South Pole and God on the North.

I didn't care for His ways so I chose my own. I found a habit or two that brought me comfort and turned to them instead of running to Him. I was utterly and absolutely miserable. My old pastor used to say, "Choose to sin, choose to suffer." That's one of the most truthful statements I've ever heard. The more you medicate your sinful lifestyle with more sin, the deeper your misery will be. Only honest repentance and truthful submission to God's ways will provide you the freedom that you're seeking and the joy you long for.

Once your vertical relationship is healed you'll be ready to deal with other people. The problem with people is that they can be mean. They say things they shouldn't say and do things they shouldn't do. They don't understand simple body language. They demand thick skin that is often missing when we're wounded. But when Christ heals our wounds, we're finally ready to face the music.

Jesus came to the Samaritan woman. He found her by the well. He refused to settle for superficial conversation and put His finger on her gaping, bleeding wound instead. He pressed until the Samaritan woman was ready to talk. He confronted her with her sins. He revealed Himself to her. Then He offered her intimacy as no one else could. He loved her with a love that is unspeakable and unconditional and unstoppable.

There's nothing as compelling as Christ's love to change us. There's nothing that will turn our lives upside down like His love. The moment we choose to surrender to His ways is the moment we're unleashed for joy. The woman "left her water jar and went away into town and said to the people, 'Come see a man who told me all that I ever did. Can this be the Christ?'" (John 4:28–29).

When Christ becomes our focus, our priorities are reordered. Our hunger is sated, and our thirst is satisfied. No longer are our physical needs our highest goal. We can let go of our water jugs and of the things we thought we desperately needed. We can finally go back to the crowd in total vulnerability and authenticity. True vulnerability is the willingness to admit to others what God already knows about who we are. The Samaritan woman no longer needed to hide. She declares triumphantly, "Come, see a man who told me all that I ever did" (v. 28). Having been completely known and still loved by Jesus, having been set free from her sin, she was ready to take off her façade and stand up to her accusers.

There's power in knowing that "There is therefore now no condemnation for those who are in Christ Jesus" (Rom. 8:1). No one can accuse you once you've been set free by the Savior. When the Judge of the world frees you of your guilt, you no longer need to hide. You are now free to love others well.

What Happens Next?

Think about it: the town whore was about to lead a revival meeting. The woman no one wanted to be around had become so compelling that everyone in town came out to see what all the fuss was about. Here's what happened:

> Many Samaritans from that town believed in him because of the woman's testimony, "He told me all that I ever did." So when the Samaritans came to him, they asked him to stay with them, and he stayed there two days. And many more believed *because of his word.* They said to the woman, "It is no longer because of what you said that we believe, for we have heard for ourselves, and we know that this is indeed the Savior of the world." (John 4:39–42, emphasis added)

When God turns your life upside down everyone will notice. The Samaritan woman suddenly had a new small group. She no longer hated church. She even joined the choir. Do you want to know the characteristics of a godly community? True community centers on a common belief that Jesus is the Light. It focuses on God's Word. It is made up of imperfect people and one perfect Savior.

The reason so many small groups and churches fail is that we forget the characteristics of true community. We minimize the importance of God's Word. We forget our common belief in a risen Savior. But mostly, we forget that we're sinners saved by grace. We expect each other to be perfect. Only Christ's love will free us to continue in authentic vulnerability and total authenticity, and therein is freedom.

You might still be hanging at the well in the heat of the day, unwilling to be seen or known. Or maybe you've encountered the Savior of the world but you refuse to let go of your jug and run back to the villagers. You might have tried it and been laughed at and ridiculed. You've decided to never again reach out to them. You're still alone. You're an expert at isolating yourself from the world.

But what if today you resolved to do whatever it takes to live in community? What if you refused to settle for selective authenticity? What if you were once again willing to be vulnerable, knowing that Christ alone is your healer, the only One who can ease the pain you might feel? You're safe to be vulnerable because of God's perfect love for you. Imagine how much fuller your life could be if you felt free enough to be yourself with the people God has put in relationship with you. Imagine how much happier you would be if you stopped hiding all the scars in your life. We spend so much time hiding our scars. Yet each one tells a story.

I'm one of those people who prefer to hide my scars. I spent three years in a small group before I felt brave enough and safe enough to sit down with my small group leader and admit my battle with lust. I was so afraid she'd look down on me and reject me. Instead, she met me with the love and the grace of the Savior. I figured if she could love me despite my scars, how much more did Christ, who died for me, truly lavish His love on me? Christ's love sets the captive free and breaks every yoke of bondage. And it is in the context of safe community that Christ's love is most deeply demonstrated and victory is claimed.

There's one more thing to consider: Who's the Samaritan woman in your life? There's a well where you live, and every day around noon someone shows up to it. That someone is waiting for you. We're living in days where people are hurting. It's easy to ignore them. It's safer to avoid them. Jesus was tired and hungry. Most normal people would have avoided Samaria. They would have chosen an easier road. But we're not normal people. We are followers of the Savior. We've been called to love when it's inconvenient and go where others won't go. The long, hard way is calling. Who will go to Samaria?

If you're looking to change your world for Christ, resolve to be vulnerable when it's easier not to. Resolve to be in community when you'd rather be alone. Resolve to love the way Jesus loved—unconditionally and selflessly. Who knows what could happen on a sunny day at noon by a well?

RESOLVED: that I will refuse to hide in isolation and intentionally choose authentic community, knowing that I have great safety and freedom in Christ's love that sets me free to love others in a way that will change my world.

Have Joy When
Life Is Depressing

Everybody wants to be happy. The United States was founded on the premise that we each have the right to life, liberty, and the pursuit of happiness. Recently a song titled "Happy" found its way to the top of the charts, selling over 5.6 million copies in the United States alone. Everybody wants to be happy. You would think Christians would want in on this concept. Instead, I grew up hearing pastors and Sunday school teachers split hairs between joy and happiness, leaving me confused and unsettled. I wanted to be happy. I couldn't understand then what I still can't understand now: If we as Christians don't have a reason to be happy, who does?

Once in a while my patients surprise me. I'll tell them their tests are normal, expecting them to be happy. Instead, they look glum, almost as if they're disappointed. Did they want to be sick? Were they hoping for an easy answer to their pain? Or are they happy and just don't know how to show it? We as followers of Christ tend to be a little bit like them. We have a hard time expressing our joy. We have convinced ourselves that we can be happy on the inside without showing it on the outside.

Perhaps you're thinking that your problems are worse than anyone else's. Perhaps you believe you've been living in the dark night of the soul longer than any of your friends have. You're constantly weighed down by your impossibly difficult circumstances. You can't help that you tend to be more melancholic to begin with. And hasn't the Bible instructed us to mourn with those who mourn anyway? Didn't God nickname one of his favorite prophets "the weeping prophet"? Do Christians have to dance in order to prove they are happy? Is it possible to *be* happy even if we don't *feel* happy? Can't we all just settle for joy and call it a day?

Few things are a more powerful testimony than joy when life's circumstances are depressing. That kind of joy cannot be faked. It is God-given, and it will change our world.

The Happiest Guy in the Bible

One of my favorite guys in the Bible is in Acts 3. He's lame, and he's a beggar. He lives in total dependence on other people's pity and kindness. I suppose he's a little pathetic, and he certainly needs help. One day, sometime after the resurrection, as Peter and John made their way to the temple for worship, this man was waiting for them. He held out his palm and asked for change. Peter, filled with the Holy Spirit, didn't have any cash but he had something far better for the beggar: "I have no silver and gold, but what I do have I give to you. In the name of Jesus Christ of Nazareth, rise up and walk!" (Acts 3:6).The man was in for a surprise. He immediately stood up and his legs were working!

His response? "And leaping up he stood and began to walk, and entered the temple with them, walking and leaping and praising God" (v. 8). Basically the guy had a dance party! He hadn't gotten what he had asked for but he was smart enough to understand that what he had received was so much more than he'd imagined. He hadn't gotten rich but he was given his whole life back. His response was the outward manifestation of an internal reality that was unencumbered by external circumstances. So he got up and he danced!

You might have every human reason to be overwhelmed. You might feel the sting of your own need. You're still waiting for God to throw a few nickels of blessing your way. Instead, Christ has given you so much more: He has given you your life back. That's reason enough to rejoice. No wonder Paul said we are to "Rejoice in the Lord always, *again* I will say, rejoice" (Phil. 4:4). Writing from a dank prison cell, Paul understood that no matter what happened on the outside, he had reason to abound with joy on the inside.

Can You Fake It Till You Make It?

In the late 1980s a group of German researchers tested the hypothesis that how we position our mouth and our facial activity could influence our mood. Participants in the study were told to hold a pen in their mouths to either mimic a smile or a frown. Turns out that turning your frown upside down, even if you don't really mean it, might increase your happy factor.

Whether or not you're a fan of behavioral psychology, you could actually test the hypothesis with a sample size of one. Go ahead and try it. No matter what you're going through right now, put a smile on your face and see what happens. It kind of works, doesn't it? It's why people who are training for sales jobs are told to smile when they get on the phone and talk to customers. A smile can change your whole outlook on life and set your mood, at least in the short term.

But our goal isn't temporary, man-made techniques for feeling better about our circumstances. What we're after is a biblical foundation for deep and enduring joy—the kind of joy that is unshaken and will change our world. Many of us have spent far too long around other Christians just like us. We have adopted the right lingo to use in small groups. We plaster a smile on our faces for the ninety obligatory minutes we are in church each week. On the outside we look like we've got it made. We talk about "how blessed we are." We romanticize our Facebook updates to make us look like one big happy machine. We tell each other that God is good, that all is well, but deep down is the sinking realization that no matter how hard we try to fake it, we're not really sure we're going to make it.

Some of us have even become a little cynical about joy and happiness. I remember reading C. S. Lewis's masterpiece *Surprised by Joy*. Lewis had spent most of his life single, and when at fifty-eight years of age he finally fell in love and married a woman named Joy, she got cancer and died four years later. Surprised by joy? I'd say he was surprised by Joy's death. Yeah, we have turned cynical about Christian joy and have no trouble understanding Sarah's eavesdropping chuckle in Genesis. A baby at her age? Ha. Her exact words were, "After I am worn out, and my lord is old, shall I have pleasure?" (Gen. 18:12).

In our hunger to satisfy our very real human desires, we have given up on the idea of pleasure. Oh, we can hang on for dear life and white-knuckle it through until heaven, but don't ask us to actually be happy—not

161

without our needs met and our expectations exceeded. As a result of our misunderstanding of enduring joy, we have lost the power of our influence in a world that is desperate for hope.

Watch Out for Joy Stealers

Many of us feel we've been handed a raw deal. We don't like our present circumstances. We think others have been given what should be ours. We want what we don't have and hate what we do have. We want what we want, and we want it right now. We are plain unhappy and we have lost our influence because of it. If we're looking to reclaim the joy that is ours in Christ, let's start by identifying these four common joy stealers.

1. The Green Monster Is Killing You

In this era of Pinterest, few quotes have been used more than this one attributed to Theodore Roosevelt: "Comparison is the thief of joy." I have a feeling you've "liked" this quote at least once in the last year. And you probably readily recognize the destructive nature of envy but you are trapped by its stronghold and it is killing you. I've been there before. My mood swings with the speed of my Facebook updates. People I haven't thought about in the last decade become my newest obsession. All of a sudden I want their vacations, their ministries, their friends, and occasionally their dogs. What often starts out as a horizontal issue soon becomes a vertical one. We begin to question God's goodness to us. We wonder why He prefers "them" over us. We become envious of them.

Envy makes our bones rot (Prov. 14:30). It brings about "disorder and every vile practice" (James 3:16). Envy caused Cain to kill his brother Abel in the first murder ever. At the root of envy is dissatisfaction with what God has given you and a desire for what others have been given. At the root of envy is a lack of trust that God is your loving Father who knows exactly what you need and when you need it.

When a patient comes in with a fishhook in his finger, it never occurs to me to simply treat the pain and send him home. I do the only thing I can do: I cut the hook out. The only way to have envy rooted out of your heart is to humbly come to God and ask Him to remove it. It will hurt, but it would kill you to keep it in. In the same way, there are some practical things we can do about the fishhooks in our lives. For me, in the case of the fishhook of social media, I've had to remove all recognizable envy triggers. From complete social media fasts to limiting the number of people I follow, I've had to get serious about cooperating with God in the battle against envy. Where is your green monster hibernating? How serious are you about uprooting this stronghold? It is not only possible but it is your only option on your journey to joy.

2. The Christian Rat Race Is Exhausting You

Have you met the Joneses yet? I'm sure you have. They go to your church and they love Jesus. In fact, they love Him just a little bit more than you do, or so it seems based on their steady stream of Christian Facebook updates. You ignore it at first, but if you're honest with yourself it bugs you and you're not even sure why. You try to one-up them. You try the "pour hot coals over their heads" approach by "liking" their statuses. It doesn't work. You keep checking what they're going to say next. It's like a drug. You know it's bad for you but you can't stop using.

I love Colossians 3:12–13 in *The Message* version of the Bible: "So, chosen by God for this new life of love, dress in the wardrobe God picked out for you: compassion, kindness, humility, quiet strength, discipline. Be even-tempered, *content with second place*, quick to forgive an offense" (emphasis added).

Aren't you tired of striving to be *numero uno*? Paul, arguably the greatest Christian who ever lived, understood the vital importance of counting others as more significant than ourselves (Phil. 2:3). He warned us not to think of ourselves more highly than we ought to think (Rom. 12:3). Paul understood that the secret to enduring joy is to drop out of the Christian rat race. This is a race you don't need to run! It's time to get over your comparisonitis. Like every good thoroughbred knows, put your blinders on and run your own race, baby.

3. Your Shattered Dreams Are Hurting You

You hoped things would turn out one way, but they didn't. Your dreams feel broken into tiny little pieces. Your joy is shaken. When you're at the crossroads of broken dreams and enduring joy, you have a decision to make: Will you trust God, the Giver of your dreams, or will you linger in self-pity and misery, trying to convince God to revive your dead dreams? Surrender is your pathway to joy. The sooner you embrace a heart that is surrendered the sooner you'll find the joy that you've lost. You can let go of your dream of a bigger house, a faster car, more friends, and a bigger platform. The most precious dream you will ever have is the one God has given you—and it's typically a dream that includes Him at the center of it.

When you get to the place where your dream controls your level of joy, that dream has become your idol. When you get to the place where you doubt God's love for you because your dream looks shattered, you might want to think about who owns your heart—your God or your idol. An idol is anything that takes the place of God in your heart. If you're aiming for joy, the only thing to do with your broken dreams is to see a chance to worship God despite your dead dream. We all have dreams. They propel us forward. They keep us hoping. They give us joy—except when they seem dead. Nothing hurts more in this life than seeing our dreams crushed, even for a season.

One of the crucial mistakes I've made is to judge God by the present condition of my dreams. When my dreams seem to thrive, I figure God is for me and that He must indeed be strong and able. But the test of faith comes when the path to our dreams look like it's swerving off course. Instead of growing in faith, we wallow in fear. It's not hard to confuse God's favor with our personalized version of the American dream. But God's favor is far bigger than that. It was God's favor that led Jesus to the cross of Calvary. It was God's favor that allowed Him to suffer so we could be free. I think you get the picture: God's favor and the American dream aren't always one and the same. But God's love for you is always the same, whether your dreams are thriving or seem to be on hold—or even if they've been buried for so long you can't even remember them.

4. Your Self-Centered Focus Is Squeezing the Life out of You

Me, me, me. It's always all about me. If you're stuck in a cycle of self-centered living, you're missing out on real joy. You've probably experienced it before. You twist your ankle and think you're going through the worst pain of your life—until you meet someone whose leg has been amputated. I was teaching about God's stripping process once and caught myself talking about how hard my life was: I had broken two engagements, hadn't been on a date in a while, and was dealing with a flooded house. All of a sudden I started laughing. Who was I kidding? My problems were minuscule compared to what most people were going through. More importantly, I had missed a critical lesson along the way, that enduring joy is found in service to others. The self-centered life will always leave us dissatisfied. True Christianity is about loving service to others in the name of Jesus.

When the lame beggar threw a dance party, those who were watching "were filled with wonder and amazement at what had happened to him" (Acts 3:10). Are people filled with wonder at the joy in your life? We are living in difficult days. People are lost and broken without Christ and they need a reason for joy. If we as resurrection people don't start living like we've got something to be happy about, our world is in real trouble. It's time to start dancing like we mean it.

Everybody Dance Now

Before there was Michael Jackson and his moonwalk, there was David dancing on the streets of Jerusalem. The occasion was the return of the ark of the Lord to its home. The ark of the Lord was a symbol of God's presence, and David was so overwhelmed with joy over its return that he was "leaping and dancing before the

Lord." (2 Sam. 6:16). His wife Michal, King Saul's daughter, wasn't impressed. In fact, she was disgusted. "How the king of Israel honored himself today," she mocked, "uncovering himself today before the eyes of his servants' female servants, as one of the vulgar fellows shamelessly uncovers himself!" (v. 20).

People who haven't been touched by God's love won't understand the joy of the Lord. David, whose life had been radically changed by God's grace, understood it well: "[I danced] before the Lord, who chose me above your father and above all his house, to appoint me as prince over Israel, the people of the Lord—and I will celebrate before the Lord. I will make myself yet more contemptible than this, and I will be abased in your eyes" (vv. 21–22).

David's response was to become even more undignified than his wife accused him of being. It didn't matter what she or anyone else thought. His heart overflowed with joy. His life was full of worship and praise. He danced with all his might, undeterred by the mockery of his wife. What was David's secret?

Give Me Back That Loving Feeling

The first time I went to Africa I was thrown for a loop. I was in one of the poorest countries on the continent. The roads weren't paved. The heat was sweltering without an air conditioner in sight. Homes—if they existed—were made of mud. Meals were cooked over an open fire and were too fly-infested for any Westerner to seriously consider eating. Shoes were scarce. Yet over and over again it became evident that nothing could stop an African from dancing. Late at night, with the flicker of candlelight illuminating the dark, one could catch the silhouettes of men, women, and children dancing the night away. We in the Western church find ourselves in the richest countries in the world and unable to capture the same sort of unshaken joy. Many theories might contribute to the Africans' joy: perhaps lower expectations of what ought to be, or the understanding that since circumstances can't change, one might as well change his or her perception of those circumstances. Whatever their reasons for joy might be, it would behoove us to learn from these Africans.

The good news is that you don't have to go all the way to Africa to learn how to dance. You can understand true and lasting joy right where you are. You *can* be happy even if it doesn't feel like you ever will. Let me refresh your joy meter by giving you four reasons for rejoicing no matter what you're going through right now.

1. This Is Not the End of the Road

Your present circumstances and life as you presently know it are not all there is. There's more. There's life beyond retirement. There's hope beyond your measly 401(k). You've been promised eternal life, and it started the moment you turned to Christ for salvation. You don't have to wait for heaven to be happy but you also don't need to try so hard to create heaven here on earth for yourself. There will come a day—hopefully soon—where we will have no more tears, no more sadness, no more pain. No matter what you're going through right now, you can stand strong, unshaken in the heat of the battle, because you know something that only a few people know: This. Is. Not. The. End.

2. Christ Is All You Really Need

You don't need more money. You don't need more sex. You don't need to lose ten pounds. (Okay, maybe you do need that.) But the things you think you so desperately need to be happy are fleeting. Christ is all you will ever really need. It took Peter a significant failure and a life-transforming meeting with Jesus to figure out that Christ is enough. It was Peter who later wrote: "[God's] divine power has granted to us all things that pertain to life and godliness" (2 Pet. 1:3). If you have Christ you have everything you need. Don't buy into the lies of the culture. Stop falling for the same marketing scams that everyone else is buying into. We typically don't believe what we haven't experienced yet. It takes a leap of faith to see what God will do with a heart that trusts Him. Are you willing to jump?

3. No One Can Ever Touch You

Satan can't harm you without God's approval. The world can't defeat you. No weapon fashioned against you will ever succeed (Isa. 54:17). In Ephesians 6 Paul tells us about the armor that God has given us to protect us. This armor is thick enough to weather any storm. Are you actively putting on your armor every morning? I'm not talking about the latest fashion trend. I'm talking of a classic that never goes out of style. It's an armor that's far stronger than you can imagine. It includes the breastplate of righteousness, the belt of truth, and shoes of peace. It comes with a shield of faith that can stop every dart the evil one throws at you. It has a fancy helmet of salvation and a sharp sword made of God's Word. It includes your prayer life, which is always giving you access to God the Father through Christ. Yeah, you are untouchable, and Christ guaranteed it with His blood. That's reason for joy.

When David went up against Goliath, King Saul gave him armor to wear. Saul thought it would protect him and help him. But David refused the man-made armor. He opted for God's armor instead. It's time for us to get rid of our man-made outfits and put on the Lord Jesus Christ instead. It's time for a total makeover!

4. You're Part of an Awesome Team

The church is God's plan for restoration and healing in this world. We—the church—are to represent

Christ's love to people who desperately need love. We are to be the hands and feet of Jesus in every corner of every country across the globe. Other Christians are not your competitors or your enemies. They are members of the same awesome team God is putting together. Everyone on this team has a different role. Picture a cathedral. Each member of the team has been given a different part in the building process. The finished cathedral is Christ's kingdom. Your part in the building process is different than mine, but each of our parts is essential to building the most beautiful cathedral the world has ever seen. This should change how you view your life and ministry, shouldn't it? It ought to rev you up to figure out exactly what your part in the cathedral building process is and do it with all your might. Others might not see or appreciate your part, but God is directing the process and He sees every bit that you do. Nothing is wasted in His economy. Every detail matters to Him.

> Since this is the kind of life we have chosen, the life of the Spirit, let us make sure that we do not just hold it as an idea in our heads or a sentiment in our hearts, but work out its implications in every detail of our lives. That means we will not compare ourselves with each other as if one of us were better and another worse. We have far more interesting things to do with our lives. Each of us is an original. . . . Make a careful exploration of who you are and the work you have

been given, and then sink yourself into that. Don't be impressed with yourself. *Don't compare yourself with others.* Each of you must take responsibility for doing the creative best you can with your own life. (Gal. 5:25–6:5 Message, emphasis added)

Those are life-giving words that will leave you unshaken if you'll start living like you believe them.

Dr. Laura Kubzansky of the Harvard School of Public Health is an expert in the field of society, human development, and health. She has spent her career studying the link between positive emotions and health and healing. In a 2007 study that followed more than six thousand men and women ages twenty-five to seventy-four, for twenty years, she found that emotional vitality—a sense of enthusiasm, hopefulness, and engagement in life, plus the ability to face life's stresses with emotional balance appears to reduce the risk of coronary heart disease. She's not the only scientist identifying this link between our happiness and our healing. Happy people live longer and their wounds heal faster. And ask any ER nurse: if nothing else, happy people are easier to take care of. So you see, it pays to be happy.

We as followers of Jesus Christ have reason for joy. We have been given good news. Our broken hearts have been healed. We've been set free. It's time we change our world by living like it. Jesus healed ten lepers in Luke 17. Only one came back "praising God with a loud voice; and he fell on his face at Jesus' feet, giving him thanks" (vv. 15–16). And he was a Samaritan at that. Jesus was amazed. "Were not ten cleansed? Where are the nine? Was no one found to return and give praise to God except this foreigner?" (vv. 17–18).

If you're looking for enduring joy, stop asking for your circumstances to change and resolve to give thanks for what you do have. It's been said that gratitude is the attitude that sets the altitude for living. You might not have accomplished your dreams yet. You might still be waiting. You might be living through unusually complex circumstances right now. You might even have reason for sadness. I'm not trying to minimize your pain in any way. But you've also been given such reason for joy. Giving thanks when we don't feel like it is an act of faith. It reflects a heart that trusts God. It yells out to a watching world that we believe God is our loving Father and He's not through with us yet. Aren't you grateful for the gift of Christ in your life? He's everything you'll ever need. He's all you'll ever want.

So what are you still waiting for? Make it your goal to put your dancing shoes on and start moving. Make it your resolution today to be grateful no matter what, to see past the circumstances you don't care for, and to refuse to settle for anything less than Christ-centered joy.

RESOLVED: that I will practice gratitude in the face of challenging circumstances and rejoice no matter what, because God is able to act above and beyond my wildest expectations, including raising my dreams from the dead.

Hope When
It Hurts Too Much

My father has end-stage kidney disease. This week we met with hospice as we're transitioning to a new normal, at least for the time being. It's been hard watching the man I have looked up to my whole life, and still do, slowly disintegrate physically. Watching him suffer hurts. Each day brings him closer to the end. As deep as our hope in Christ is, this pain is very real. Hope for healing on this side of eternity has dwindled for my dad. Few things are as powerful as hanging on to hope when hope looks dead. Few things inspire us like watching people who keep on hoping despite the pain of their dead dreams. When our dreams look dead and the road seems blocked, it's easy to lose hope. In order to stand strong in a culture used to giving up, we as followers of Jesus Christ must resolve to maintain hope even when life feels hopeless and our pain is great.

Aron Ralston. You might not immediately be familiar with his name, but I bet you've heard of the twenty-seven-year-old climber who got his arm stuck while hiking in a canyon. Instead of quietly dying in his trap, the young man, later played by James Franco in the movie *127 Hours*, cut off his own arm in order to save his life. Somehow Aron was able to fight for hope and embrace the pain in his life, and ultimately rise above it.

Stories like Aron's are not unique. In the bestselling book *Unbroken*, author Lauren Hillenbrand tells the story of a young lieutenant in the Second World War, Louis Zamperini, who survived forty-seven days on a raft in the Pacific Ocean and then later was captured and tortured by the enemy—and still made it home a year and a day after his disappearance. The words on *Unbroken*'s cover inspire even the most cynical hearts: "Driven to the limits of endurance, Zamperini would answer desperation with ingenuity; suffering with hope, resolve, and humor; brutality with rebellion. His fate, whether triumph or tragedy, would be suspended on the fraying wire of his will."

Of course, Lauren Hillenbrand understands a little bit about pain and endurance herself, as she has suffered for years with what she describes as a "sudden illness" that has left her physically incapacitated. When

asked about the irony of writing about physical challenges while living through her own painful ordeal,
Hillenbrand said, "I'm looking for a way out of here. I
can't have it physically, so I'm going to have it intellectually. . . . And it's just fantastic to be there alongside
Louie as he's breaking the NCAA mile record. People
at these vigorous moments in their lives—it's my way
of living vicariously."[1]

Then there's Nick Vujicic, a man without limbs.
This Australian Christian evangelist was born without
arms and legs and has overcome mental and emotional obstacles to become a modern-day hero. He now
spends his life motivating others to hope, overcome
their pain, and live a life of impact and power no matter what they're facing.

We are inspired by the real-life examples of men
and women who have felt pain in its most excruciating
forms and have been able to rise above it with unstoppable hope. How is it that while so many are crushed
by their pain, some are able to remain unshaken and
strong in the face of their own personal torment?

Hope through Tears

And what of Christians and pain? Are Christians im-
mune to pain and suffering? Anyone who has followed

1. Lauren Hillenbrand, "A Sudden Illness," *The New Yorker* (July 7, 2003),
56, http://www.newyorker.com/magazine/2003/07/07/a-sudden-illness.

Jesus Christ for more than a minute knows that pain is an integral part of the Christian life. Is it possible for us, as followers of Jesus, to keep on hoping despite great pain? If you've read even a few pages of Scripture you cannot overlook the stunning presence of pain as part of our journey with and toward Christ. Yet in those same pages we read some of the most empowering promises.

- "We are more than conquerors through him who loved us." (Rom. 8:37)
- "He who is in you is greater than he who is in the world." (1 John 4:4)
- "This is the victory that has overcome the world—our faith." (5:4)
- "We are afflicted in every way, but not crushed; perplexed, but not driven to despair; persecuted, but not forsaken; struck down, but not destroyed." (2 Cor. 4:8–9)
- "I can do all things through him who strengthens me." (Phil. 4:13)

God pours out His words through the Scriptures, like a motivational book for the ages, reminding us that we follow a Savior who has defeated death and destroyed sin and its power over us. Over and over again God uses the broken, the battered, the lowly, the seemingly defeated, the prisoners, the uneducated, the hurting, and the needy. They rise above their

circumstances and soar. Christ Himself, the Captain
of our salvation, was made perfect through suffering
(Heb. 2:10). Born in a manger as the son of a lowly car-
penter, He later turned the world upside down through
His life, death, and resurrection. But before the cross
and before the resurrection first came Gethsemane.
It was in the garden of Gethsemane that Jesus felt the
most excruciating pain and overcame it. Our Savior
not only understands our pain but identifies with us
in it completely. We worship a Savior who has felt our
deepest pain. He sympathizes with our weaknesses
because of His own firsthand experience. He yearns
to give us comfort when we need it.

To live defeated by our pain is not our destiny as
followers of Jesus Christ. He gave His life to ensure
our victory. To live overcome by our circumstances is
to misunderstand who Jesus is and what He has done
for us. Christ never promised us a pain-free life. The
fact is that pain is real. We hurt, and for good reason.
People lose their homes in earthquakes and hurricanes.
They lose their sons and daughters to sex traffickers.
They lose their lives to hunger, water shortage, cancer, and heart disease. Whether it's natural disasters
or life-ending diseases, violence at the hand of evil or
global injustice, our pain is real and it's deep. Life is
hard. The pain we feel is acute, and it spares no one
in this world. What makes the Christian life radical
isn't that we escape pain but that we can rise above it
through Christ and the strength He gives us. What

distinguishes the life of Christ's followers isn't the absence of pain but how we respond to the pain in our lives and how we react under pressure when the pain is so severe that we can hardly breathe. Our pain reflects the victorious reality of the resurrection.

Wouldn't it be nice if we could take a pill to make the pain go away? But things are never that simple. Some days feel like torture, and it hurts. Motivational speakers try to teach us to use positivity to overcome our pain. But I've found myself in places in my life where no amount of positive mental thinking will work me out of my pit of despair. When I'm in that place where I cannot motivate myself with positive self-talk and positive energy, I realize that there has to be more. The good news is that we have more than just positive thinking. We have a living hope in Christ. We have an anchor for our souls. We have a way through the pain. That way has a name: Jesus Christ, our risen Savior.

Hope Is More
Than a Positive Mental Attitude

God has given us far more than positivity. He's given us His Son who demonstrated victory by rising from the dead. He's given us His Spirit to enable us to live out the Christian life the way He lived out His: victoriously and triumphantly. His plan is for us to live in such a victorious way that by doing so we bring His kingdom here to this earth. We are to be ambassadors of the kind of powerful living that shakes our world and culture. We ought to stick out in our ability to rise above our circumstances. Yet so many of us are failing. I'm embarrassed to tell you how often I've crumbled under the pressure of pain. This crumbling reveals itself in a variety of shapes and forms in my life: misplaced anger, impatient frustration, whining and complaining, and once in a while, the pit of self-pity and even a few potholes of despair. But this is not the end of the story.

Where God Puts a Comma

It was a seven-mile walk from Jerusalem to Emmaus, and on that day the walk felt like an interminable journey of sorrow. The two disciples were weighed down by their pain. They had expected God to do the impossible. They had expected the Messiah to take over the world. They had expected victory and success and at the very least a natural death instead of a painful and shameful crucifixion. It was the worst day of their lives.

Suddenly a man came walking up alongside them and struck up a conversation. The man was Jesus risen from the dead, but the disciples had not been given the ability to recognize Him yet. My guess is that at that point they didn't feel like talking but were too polite to ignore Him. "Are you the only visitor to Jerusalem who does not know the things that have happened there in these days?" they wondered (Luke 24:18). Then they told Him what they were talking about: "Jesus of Nazareth, a man who was a prophet mighty in deed and word before God and all the people, and how our chief priests and rulers delivered him up to be condemned to death, and crucified him" (vv. 19–20).

But the worst was yet to come. The disciples then uttered three fatal words of defeat that were the nail on the coffin of their pain: "But we had hoped that he was the one to redeem Israel" (v. 21).

We. Had. Hoped.

Have you ever uttered these three words of hopelessness, not knowing that victory was already on the way? Have you ever misinterpreted the most painful event in your life without any idea of the miracle God was already working out on your behalf? I can't keep track of the times that I've given up on God and twisted things around in my head and assumed that my pain was final, that I'd been defeated, while all along God was walking right next to me, preparing the victory for me. You too? The disciples on the road to Emmaus had put a period where God had put a comma. They had written off the Lord when God hadn't even started yet. They had sunk into despair when hope was on the way.

It's easy to talk about the life that's unshaken when everything is going well. People flocked to Jesus when He fed the five thousand and cured diseases. It was at the cross that everyone fled. The closer Jesus got to the cross the thinner the crowds became, and eventually even His closest friends fled. That's what pain will do. It tests our mettle. It crystallizes what we really believe. Anyone can boast in the Lord when their dreams have come true and their prayers have been answered. The challenge is to stand strong when life is hard, to hope when hope looks dead. The key is to live victoriously when everything screams against it.

As an ER doctor I think in lists, and when it comes to pain, there are four things I know for sure:

- Pain exists.
- Pain has a cause.
- Pain can be treated but it's far better to treat its cause.
- Pain doesn't have to define you.

We can talk about the resurrection until we're blue in the face, but the way to show if we really believe it is by watching how we respond to the pain in our lives. What will define you: your pain or God's Word? Are you willing to settle for a Band-Aid while the internal bleeding is killing you, or are you committed to identifying the cause of your bleeding and going after it with a vengeance?

Five Painkillers You Can Use

How do you hang on to hope when you're in pain? How do you hold on with resolve to God's Word when you feel crushed by the weight of your circumstances? When it comes to using the pain in your life as fuel for godliness, here are a few tools you can use for victorious living.

1. Lighten Up on the Clichés

"It's going to hurt me more than it's going to hurt you." "No pain no gain." "If it doesn't kill you, it makes you stronger." "Pain is your friend." I'm not a huge fan of clichés. Clichés are nothing more than old-fashioned tweets. Here today, gone tomorrow. Pithy quotes might motivate us for a minute, but their effect is short-lived. What we need is life change. What I long for is the transformed, powerful life that Christ promised us. Don't you? We need upside-down, inside-out radical living that no litany of clichés will produce but is rightfully ours in Christ Jesus by faith. Clichés are easy to remember and to retweet, but what we desperately need to strengthen our resolve to live with hope is God's Word. The more of God's Word that we hide in our hearts, the more it will give us strength when we need it the most.

2. Let Go of the Blame Game

When a kid comes into the ER with a cut, families get caught up in how it happened and whose fault it was. The truth is that it doesn't matter who did what. There's a cut, and it hurts, and it must be fixed. When Adam and Eve sinned, Adam blamed Eve and Eve blamed the serpent, but the fact remains that all of us humans are still suffering because of it today. Instead of blaming each other, Adam and Eve should have acknowledged their wrong and accepted God's mercy, then adapted to their new normal outside of Eden. When Job went through his painful trials, his wife begged him to blame God and his friends blamed him for his own problems. Unlike Adam and Eve, Job was innocent and had done nothing to deserve his pain, yet the blame game was just as much a part of Job's story as it was for our first parents. Blaming someone else for our pain is natural and gives us a temporary sense of control. It might even help us come up with an explanation for the pain. But it doesn't work. What works far better than the blame game is recognizing God's sovereign control over our lives. It's understanding that God didn't find Adam and Eve in the garden to shame them but rather to cover them. It's accepting Christ's forgiveness for our sin. It's extending that same forgiveness to those who seem to be the cause of our pain.

3. Get off the Self-Pity Train

Self-pity is endemic. It is defined as a self-indulgent attitude concerning our hardships. The problem with self-pity is that it believes it's been wronged. It's the notion that God hasn't given you what you deserve and that you've somehow been overlooked and forgotten. Self-pity is an attitude that dislocates a Christian from a sovereign God who is behind every detail and circumstance of your life.

Charles Spurgeon once said, "God is too good to be unkind. He is too wise to be confused. If I cannot trace His hand, I can always trust His heart." The biggest lie that Satan will throw your way is that God doesn't care about you anymore, and self-pity slowly feeds that lie. In 1 Peter 5:7 we're told the truth: "[Cast] all your anxieties on him, because he cares for you." God does care about you. He knows each and every hair on your head. He's a God who knows you so well and still loves you so much. The self-pity train can kill you if you don't guard against its lies with the truth of God's Word. It's time you jump off that train and run toward grace.

4. Bury Your Past at the Cross

Paul killed Christians before he became a Christ-follower. Yet God used Paul to write the bulk of the New Testament and to build the church. Crazy? You better believe it. So how did Paul deal with his past? His solution was to bury his past at the foot of the cross: "Forgetting what lies behind and straining forward to what lies ahead, I press on toward the goal for the prize of the upward call of God in Christ Jesus" (Phil. 3:13–14). Onward and upward. Does Satan taunt you with your past? As St. Teresa of Avila is credited with saying, "When Satan reminds you of your past, remind him of his future." Remind him that Christ buried your past at the cross. Are you afraid someone will find out something that hasn't come out already? Christ already knows it, and He loved you enough to die for you in spite of it. You have nothing to hide anymore. Have you failed miserably and repeatedly in the past? It's time to get rid of the Rolodex of sin. Failure is the best teacher you'll ever find. Learn from it, then let it go. Your past might be part of who you are but it has no power over you. Use it to rejoice in God's mercy and grace and move onward and upward. Use it as your platform to highlight God's love and grace and watch God use your past to change your world like He did with the apostle Paul!

5. Leave Your Fears to God

Pain and fear are often inseparable. *What if I don't make it through it? What if I never find relief? What if God doesn't come through for me?*

What is it that you are afraid of? Are you afraid of what your pain will reveal about you? God's plan isn't to hurt you through your pain but to shape you through it (Prov. 25:4). Like a perfect potter, He works and reworks the clay until it seems good to Him (Jer. 18:4). He molds the clay until it reflects the beauty He is after. This process is called sanctification. It's God's work in you through your pain to make you more Christlike. It's a work that is utterly dependent on the Holy Spirit in you. It's a work that God started the moment you gave your life to Him and is committed to complete when you finally see Jesus face-to-face. Are you afraid that things aren't going to get better? They will. I love 2 Timothy 1:7. "For God gave us a spirit not of fear but of power and love and self-control." You've quoted it many times before. It's time to embrace it.

When All Else Fails

I've already mentioned David a few times in this book. Before he became the greatest king of Israel, David went through many trying times. In a particularly dark season, David had to learn to deal with some serious pain in his life. Let me give you some background.

David was on the run. Samuel the prophet had died, and King Saul hated David so much that David had to move into a cave for a while. His friends were few, and oddly included some Philistines, who were the sworn enemies of Israel. That's how bad things looked for David. But they were about to get worse. David came home from a trip to find that the Amalekites had raided his town and taken captive all the women and children. To make matters worse, the Amalekites had burned down the entire town. Nothing was left.

And when David and his men came to the city, they
found it burned with fire, and their wives and sons
and daughters taken captive. Then David and the
people who were with him raised their voices and
wept until they had no more strength to weep. (1 Sam.
30:3–4)

David and his men were in excruciating pain. What
do you do when life and tragedy collide? How do
you respond to this kind of devastating pain in your
life? David's men wanted to stone him. They felt
bad for themselves and blamed David for their pain.
Imagine the weight of it. Try to feel what David was
going through. Here's a man who thought God had
chosen him to be the next king of Israel. Instead, he
was living in a cave and his own men were turning
against him.

Where do you go when your pain becomes this
severe? Millions of Americans make their way to the
ER for pain relief when faced with the bitter reality of
pain. Some get temporary rest—until the next wave
of pain hits. Still others get pretty good at numbing
their pain with the anesthetic du jour. They do it
with food or drugs or sex or mindless entertainment.
It works for a while, until the pain gets too loud and
deafening.

David couldn't numb his pain, and he had no way
to treat it. He was beyond the point of workable
human strategy. His back was against the wall and

he was desperate. So he did the only thing he could do. "David was greatly distressed, for the people spoke of stoning him, because all the people were bitter in soul, each for his sons and daughters. *But David strengthened himself in the LORD his God*" (v. 6, emphasis added).

There comes a time in your life when nothing will do but God Himself. There comes a time in your life when only the Lord can make sense out of your pain and confusion. Only He can rescue you. Only He understands the depth of your pain.

When the disciples on the road to Emmaus had lost hope, Jesus rebuked them: "O foolish ones, and slow of heart to believe all that the prophets have spoken! Was it not necessary that the Christ should suffer these things and enter into his glory?" (Luke 24:25–26). He then started with Moses and worked His way through the Scriptures to get them back on track.

Life is never as hopeless as we make it out to be. We are never as alone as we feel. Things are never as unclear as we think. If we look at the facts too long without a measure of faith, we will sink into despair, and the only way to build our faith is through the living Word of God. When you look at the painful facts in your life through the lens of God's promises you will find hope for the future. The truth is that without suffering there is no glory, without death there is no resurrection, and without pain there is no victory.

Purpose in Our Pain

Some people love the birthing process. I'm not one of them. It took me one night on call in obstetrics to know that my calling was not to deliver babies. The pain is excruciating. The agony is palpable. Every two hours I would find myself checking the cervix of a woman still writhing in pain, her sweat soaking the sheets. I couldn't take it. Eventually, her pain only got worse. Her moans grew louder. Her pushing became more rhythmic. For a few minutes I thought I would die, and I wasn't even the one having the baby. And then like magic, the crowning of a head, the appearance of a shoulder, and then the feet slipped out.

Finally, after what felt like an interminable night of pain, morning came with relief and rejoicing. Ask any mother in the world: in that moment, all the pain, all the agony, all the discomfort is forgotten at the sight of the little bundle of joy. I don't know where you are in your own birthing process. You might be just starting to feel the pain in your life, or you might be in the middle of the most painful contractions you've ever felt. You long for relief. I'm here to tell you that it's coming. Relief is on the way.

In 2 Corinthians, Paul shares a secret. He reminds us of the blessing of pain.

Blessed be the God and Father of our Lord Jesus Christ, the Father of mercies and God of all comfort, who comforts us in all our affliction, so that we may be able to comfort those who are in any affliction, with the comfort with which we ourselves are comforted by God. (2 Cor. 1:3–4)

This is a secret that some doctors understand better than others. Once in a while I see a patient who has an ovarian cyst and is going through what she describes as the worst pain of her life. I look her in the eyes and tell her one of the most powerful things I can tell someone. I say, "I know what you're going through. When I was eight years old, I had an ovarian cyst that became infected and I had to have surgery for it."

Suddenly I'm much more than just her doctor. I'm her partner in her pain. I'm someone who understands, someone who feels, someone who cares because I've been there too.

Are you willing to let God use your pain to someday help someone else who is hurting? Are you willing to endure knowing that your experience might just save someone else? If you're looking to impact your world, resolve to let God use your pain and embrace the power of suffering.

As I'm writing this, I am in Arizona. In July. It's over 100 degrees outside and that's a whole lot of hot for a Chicago girl. Every afternoon I take a break from writing to go on a hike. Every day I figure this is the day I'm going to keel over and die. But I persist. I push through the pain and step after step I have climbed higher and scaled more ground than I ever thought possible. I am not the fittest or the strongest girl climbing the Arizona mountains, but I'm making it to the summits and I am having fun. Sometimes in life you have to just push through the pain to see how far you can go.

My cancer patients amaze me. Prick after prick, and chemo round after chemo round, they show up to the ER with a fever and a smile on their face. Step-by-step, they push through their pain toward victory. Some get the victory they want and some don't, but all give it their best. We as followers of Jesus Christ have a secret: we are already victorious. Our steps are never wasted. Our efforts are never in vain. That's reason enough to push through our pain. As we surrender our pain to God we'll find in Him the comfort we're seeking and the strength we long for.

Few things will change our world like our resolve to hope when it hurts too much. Few things will radically transform our world like our resolve to believe God when everything screams against Him. Hope has a way of showing up when we're not looking for it. When it does, anything can happen.

RESOLVED: that I will anchor my life on the hope of Christ's resurrection even when life hurts too much, because I know that God is in control of every detail of my life, and I am certain of His unstoppable love for me.

Rest in the Midst of Chaos

One of the greatest gifts God has given us is the gift of rest. He gives us peace in the storm. Yet most of us are intent on living in the chaos.

You know what I mean when I talk about chaos. Chaos is the minivan that you're afraid to open the door to because you're not sure what will fall out. Chaos is the state of your house when that unexpected guest rings your doorbell, and you hide in the closet hoping they'll just go away and come back in a decade or two. Chaos is the ER waiting room on a Monday night in winter. Chaos is your state of mind the second your eyes open, and you're fully aware of every need of every person in your family and every meal you'll need to prepare and every task your boss wants you to accomplish and every bill you need to pay and your feet haven't even hit the floor yet. Chaos is the overwhelming overflow of negative thoughts that deluge your mind as a single person on a quiet Friday night at home.

In other words, chaos is a typical day in the typical life of the typical Christian. But we can be busy without being chaotic. Our days could be packed and not feel out of control. After all, Jesus was busy. His days were jam-packed with ministry and people and demands. Our aim isn't to take a vacation to a peaceful destination and refuse to come back as the means to escape chaos. What is far better is to resolve to find rest in the midst of our chaos. Our aim is to maintain joy in this life and maximize our impact in this world regardless of how hectic our days threaten to be. It is possible. And it all starts when we agree to let go of what we think should happen in our lives and yield to God's perfect place for us: the place of quiet trust.

Hello, Anyone There?

Shortly after my first book came out, my close friends would tell you I was a bit of a mess. I had really wanted it to be a bestseller. I had prayed it would be a bestseller. I had dreamed it would be a bestseller. I willed it to jump up to the bestseller list. The book didn't even make it to the shelf at Barnes and Noble.

I was disappointed (aka devastated, but that's too embarrassing to admit in public).

My response was to work harder at making it happen. I tweeted more, begged more friends to buy it, blogged more about it, and even bought ten extra copies of it myself to help speed up the process. It was utter chaos, and it didn't work. After a month I was exhausted. Perhaps the storm was of my own doing, but where, I wondered, was the Holy Spirit's power to take my book from its meager, average existence to a higher ground of greater usefulness for the kingdom? One day, when I least expected it, God spoke to me about it.

It was a typical midsummer morning—a morning filled with questions and anxieties. I made my usual cup of black coffee and sat down at my desk with my Bible open but little expectation of the divine showing up. It's not that I didn't want Him to show up. It's that I had grown too numb with my own "impress God with my Bible reading plan" strategy to notice the divine.

On that particular morning I opened my Bible to 1 Kings 18 and read a story I had read a million times before: Elijah at Mount Carmel. In a brilliant account of the miraculous, this hairy man of God took on every idol worshiper of his day and won. God showed up with fire from heaven and it was mind-boggling and awesome.

And reading about it depressed me.

I had dreamed about this kind of thing happening in my own life. I had prayed for it and hungered for it. Why, despite my deep desire to see God's glory, had my life come short of anything remotely close to this kind of magnificent display of the Almighty? Why did others seem to see God show up in ways that I simply watched from afar?

The few times I spoke my frustrations out loud to people they would tell me to stop complaining and be grateful for what God was already doing in my life. I was grateful. I did see. But I wanted more. I was at a significant crossroads in my life. Would God show Himself mighty on my behalf or not? And if He didn't, was it because He couldn't, or wouldn't? And would my life still stand unshaken even if God never brought down fire in my life—ever?

The more I pondered these questions the more bereft I felt. Intellectually, I knew the answers. I knew that Christ had risen from the dead for me, and I could jot down pages worth of all the great things God had done for me, but I wanted more. I wanted fire from heaven. I was looking for a God big enough to exceed my imagination but caring enough to see me right here, right now in my point of need. I was hungry for a God who could manage all of my day-to-day stuff in addition to answering my growing list of questions, questions that I was becoming too afraid to ask out loud.

The more I thought about Elijah on Mount Carmel, the madder I got. How did Elijah get to that place of power? Had I missed a step somewhere? I obsessed over the passage for days. Surely there was a secret I had missed, a magic potion, a specific prayer, a ritual, something that would unleash God's power in my life.

And then I saw it.

It all started in 1 Kings 17. The first time we hear the name Elijah is the day he shows up to King Ahab's court to predict a drought. Here's this small-town kid from Tishbe making a play in the big leagues. More surprisingly, his prediction turns out to be accurate. Suddenly he's a superstar. If he were living in today's world, he'd be placed on the cover of every magazine and making his rounds on every morning talk show. His Twitter feed would explode and he'd be offered a mega book deal: the rock 'n' roll prophet from Tishbe. Instead, God sends him away. It's hard to believe but it's true: "Depart from here and turn eastward and hide yourself by the brook Cherith, which is east of the Jordan. You shall drink from the brook, and I have commanded the ravens to feed you there. So he went and did according to the word of the LORD" (1 Kings 17:3–5).

Cherith. Seriously? Elijah takes a risk for God, puts himself out there, and God sends him to Cherith in the middle of nowhere to drink from a brook in a time of drought and be fed by a bird? Why in the world would God do that?

God Works in Mysterious Ways

God never ceases to amaze me. In the place where we might expect accolades and a bigger platform, God tells Elijah to slow down and listen. I gradually began to understand. If God was ever going to use me at Mount Carmel, I was going to have to be willing to spend some time in my very own Cherith. The word *cherith* means "a cutting off." It is a place where you might find yourself alone and cut off from the crowd, with no one to turn to but God. It is a place of quiet dependence and growing trust. For weeks I tried to resist it. I even tried to fake the silence. I turned the music off and went for walks alone.

"I *am* listening," I would argue. "I've quit trying so hard," I would proclaim.

But deep in my soul I hadn't acknowledged what was becoming more and more evident to anyone watching: my mind wasn't quiet. My spirit wasn't still. And God's plan was to lovingly send me deeper into my Cherith, where I could once again get acquainted with His presence in my life. Unlike Elijah, though, I didn't go quietly. I went kicking and screaming, but God still got the job done. He plopped me in my Cherith and held me tight until I finally settled down.

There is a crazy contraption in the ER called a "papoose board." It's a blue Velcro board that holds kids down against their will in order to still them long enough for me to fix their problems. Just about every single kid I've ever cared for in the ER hates it. Over and over again I catch myself telling my patients to either sit still or it's papoose time. The kids are typically too upset to cooperate, so there comes a point when I stop negotiating and lovingly but forcefully wrap the kids in the papoose in order to fix them up.

If you are a follower of Jesus Christ you have two choices: cooperate with God and learn to be still, or realize that God is going to help you get there. It's up to you to choose to either quietly trust Him or go down kicking and screaming. God is too loving to keep you where you're at simply because you don't want to go where you need to.

The summer my first book came out began with me doing a lot more talking than listening. That summer I quit my job as director of the women's ministry at my church so that I could launch my career as speaker/writer extraordinaire. That summer my house flooded in a near total disaster. By fall I endured yet another blow: I left my church home after nearly a decade of serving there. I felt alone, heartbroken, and discouraged. I had run out of options. In a place of utter dependence all I could do was look up for God's raven, morning by morning, for a fresh piece of bread to carry me through the day. For the first time in my life I found myself cut off from my usual connections and ability to network, cut off from the very platform I thought God had worked so hard to build around me, and cut off from my own noisy attempts at getting something amazing accomplished for God.

Have you ever found yourself in your very own Cherith? You expected to see fire come down from heaven, but instead you catch yourself staring at your reflection in a drying brook day after day, wondering what went wrong in your life. You wonder where the Holy Spirit is. You wonder about the life of power you thought God would manifest in and through you. You don't feel strong. You're shaking in your boots. You don't feel successful. You feel you've disappointed the Holy Spirit. And eventually after arguing, and fighting, and resisting, you're out of words, you're out of ideas, you're out of options.

So you finally stop long enough to listen.

The Power of Quiet Surrender

For most of us Cherith is unfamiliar territory and it's a little bit shaky at first. You feel forgotten and isolated. You check your pulse and confirm that you're still breathing. You're alive. Summer turns into fall, and slowly Isaiah 30:15 takes on new meaning: "In returning and rest you shall be saved; in quietness and in trust shall be your strength." You start to believe it.

There is a weird phenomenon in pediatrics called a "breath-holding spell." It's scary and will often land a kid in the ER. If you're a parent and have witnessed it you know what I mean by scary. When a willful toddler can't get her own way she starts crying so loud and so hard that she will actually quit getting fresh oxygen into her lungs. For a split second, the toddler will turn blue and go limp. Occasionally the toddler might even seize or stop breathing. For a brief moment, the kid looks dead. But she is not dead. As a matter of fact, breath-holding spells are benign. When parents ask me how they can prevent them, I tell them it's a piece of cake: teach your kid to slow down and listen. I know what you're thinking: I clearly don't have any kids of my own!

If you've ever wondered why some Christians see more of God's power in their lives than others, it's not as complicated as you might think. Christians who understand God's power have learned the importance of their Cherith. They have learned to find rest in the midst of the chaos. They have learned to yield. They have learned the power of quiet surrender.

I've always yearned for God-sized breakthroughs in my life and imagined them to be in the big acts, like fire coming down from heaven. I want God to reveal Himself in big ways in my life. I suppose I have used quiet surrender as leverage for what I want from God. If I could just surrender every little detail in my life to Him, maybe He'd finally show up in the big ways

I longed for. But I'm learning that breakthrough is far more than fire coming down from heaven. Breakthrough is the daily patience to endure the drudgery of yet another day in the drought. Breakthrough is the daily willingness to eat the same bread morning after morning and night after night. Breakthrough is the ability to sing praises when you feel forgotten. It's the determination not to lose hope when your dreams seem broken and hope seems distant.

Breakthrough is that moment when we see Jesus asleep in the midst of our storms and still trust that He hasn't forgotten us, that He's still in control. Much like us, the disciples lacked that kind of quiet trust. They panicked when the storm hit. They saw the waves and freaked out. They felt the wind and hollered. When they saw that Jesus was asleep, they were dismayed. "Do you not care that we are perishing?" they accused Him. Jesus was unfrazzled. "Why are you so afraid? Have you still no faith?" He asked (Mark 4:38, 40). Then He quieted the storm with just a word. This was new territory for the disciples. They thought they knew who Jesus was, but this was a whole new dimension of His deity. "Who then is this, that even the wind and the sea obey him?" they marveled (v. 41). Even the winds and the waves obey Him. Breakthrough is the realization that no storm can steal your peace, no hurricane can rob your joy, no chaos can break your rest when Jesus is in the boat with you. It's an awakening to who God is and the willingness to fling yourself in unflinching trust onto Him, knowing that even the winds and the waves will do what He wants.

Sin is getting what I want, when I want it, in the way I want it without considering what God wants and trusting Him for it. When that happens, our hearts become restless and we stop being quiet. Our hearts become chaotic. At the root of our troubles is a heart that is not yet trained to trust God. We don't believe God. Cherith is the place God wants to teach us to trust Him. It's a place of helplessness where we are finally forced to turn to Him in complete dependence. Cherith is our place for breakthrough.

Elijah's story didn't end at Cherith. Do you want to know what happened to Elijah after living by the Cherith for a while? In 1 Kings 17:7–9 it says, "After a while the brook dried up, because there was no rain in the land. Then the word of the LORD came to him, 'Arise, go to Zarephath, which belongs to Sidon, and dwell there. Behold, I have commanded a widow there to feed you.'"

One would think that God would honor the obedience and humility of His servants with some positivity. Instead, things have a way of initially going from bad to worse. After Elijah had hung out by the brook for a while, it went dry! So God moved him to Zarephath, to live with a poor widow who could barely support herself. No respectable man of God at that time would deign to live with a widow in South Lebanon, yet that's exactly where God sent Elijah. Are you following the pattern here? Before Elijah could begin to see fire at Mount Carmel, he had to learn dependence in a place of need and humility in a place of obscurity. It was at Cherith that Elijah's faith grew. It was at Zarephath that Elijah raised the widow's son from the dead. It was in her upper room that Elijah learned to pray with power.

Are you looking for breakthrough in your life? Do you dream of moments where God will show up in your life with all His might and His power? The secret to powerful living is to surrender to God in the places where you feel most needy and broken. God has put you in a place of need in order to teach you to trust Him. He does it not because He's forgotten you but because He loves you deeply. As long as you continue to argue with your Great Physician and try to do things on your own, it will be hard for you to receive His healing. It's time to stop kicking and screaming and resolve to find rest in the midst of chaos.

Silence Stealers and Quiet Seekers

What keeps you from a quiet heart? What hinders your hearing?

Is it the Killer Ds: too many distractions, the pain of defeat, and the reality of disasters? Is it the Awful Es: electronics that need leashes, entertainment that needs policing, and extras that you don't really need in your life? Or maybe you're just too busy with your work and too focused on your mission.

You're too obsessed with your hobbies.

You're too intent on getting your way.

You're too proud to admit you've been wrong or need help.

You're too opinionated. You think you know what's best.

You're too rushed for quiet.

You're too afraid of what you'll hear.

You're too demanding, too ungrateful, too preoccupied with your problems, too worried about the outcome.

You're too stiff-necked to humble yourself and admit you need to change.

You're too steeped in sin, too rebellious for correction, too hung up on your habits.

You turn to prayer as a last resort. You're chasing after the wind, constantly discontent. You resent God and His ways, you doubt that His Word is true. You don't believe He loves you. What is it that's obstructing your heart from the stillness that welcomes the Almighty? What's your excuse for not resting long enough to stop, look, and listen? What accounts for all the noise in your life?

It's time to declutter. It's time to detox. Some things have to go. This is serious business. You might need to destroy your television and annihilate your phone. You might need to break up with your boyfriend or kick your roommate out for a while. You might have to sell your boat or give away your golf clubs. You might need to kick fear in the face. I have to tell my patients over and over again, "If your kid has asthma, you need to quit smoking." They make excuses. "We only smoke outside," they'll say. Secondhand smoke will kill your kid too. How far are you willing to go for your healing? To what extreme will you go for the life that's unshaken?

The summer of my Cherith threatened to be the worst summer of my life, but it turned out to be the best. If you're longing for breakthrough in your life, and want to see the power of the Holy Spirit move mightily in your life, then it's time to make a change. It's time to recognize the noise in your soul. It's time to leave the chaos of the crowd and find a drying brook for yourself somewhere. If you're a quiet seeker, I want to let you in on four little secrets.

1. It's More Than Just a Time and Place

When Christians think of having a quiet heart, they automatically think of their quiet time. For years now the followers of Jesus Christ have described the time they spend with the Lord each morning as their "quiet time." They whip out a journal, grab a pen, close their eyes, and then get frustrated when God doesn't speak to them in the allotted time they have given Him for the day. Although I firmly believe in setting a daily time to spend with God each day, having a quiet heart is much more than keeping a quiet time. Developing a specific time that you give to God each day is a great and necessary step to listening to God. But true rest cannot be found in checking an item off your to-do list or by going through the motions of reading your Bible. The kind of rest you're looking for is only found in the person of Jesus Christ (Heb. 4:1–10). It happens by faith when you get on your knees and desperately seek His face. He is your resting place no matter how busy your schedule gets and no matter where you find yourself in the course of a day.

2. There Are No Exceptions to the Rule

Jesus took time away from the crowd and prayed. The disciples prayed. Great men and women of God over the centuries prayed. David Brainerd died at age twenty-nine and did more for God in his brief life than most of us will ever dream of. In his diary, he wrote, "I love to live alone in my own little cottage, where I can spend much time in prayer." Martin Luther is said to have spent an hour with God each morning, doubling that time on particularly hard days. If you want to live unshaken, you're going to have to plan your time with God. You're going to have to fight for it in an age of distractions. You're going to have to protect your time with God and accept that some will mock and misunderstand you. No matter how hectic your life may be, this is a battle worth fighting. You might even have to escape to the bathroom for your quiet in the storm. God isn't too picky about where you meet Him. He'll talk to you anywhere and at any hour. Where there's a will, God will make a way.

3. Practice Makes Perfect

Many people get frustrated too quickly by their time with God. They complain that they don't hear anything. They don't see anything happening during that time. God often reveals Himself in unexpected and unplanned ways, but typically He reveals Himself through His Word. So open it up and eat it slowly. Remember that practice makes perfect. Lean in and learn to listen. Instead of rushing through your daily Bible passage and patting yourself on the back for being on-target in your YouVersion plan, meditate on a single verse from God's Word from time to time. Be present with the Lord during your time with Him. Every once in a while my mom will call me while I'm busy doing other things. She'll talk for a while. I'll answer for a while. It's only after I hang up that I notice I have no idea what my mom said or how she is really doing. A wasted conversation is one where you're listening but not hearing. Hearing God with the intent to obey takes time and practice.

4. Be in It for the Long Haul

We tend to overestimate what God wants to do through us in the short run and underestimate what

He wants to do in us through a lifetime of faithfulness and obedience. It's high time we get over our obsession with immediate results and commit to persevering to the end no matter what. Some of my patients give up on their treatment only two days after starting a course of antibiotics. When they come back to the ER, unimproved, and I discover the problem, I explain to them that they will not get better if they don't stick the treatment out to the end. I also warn them that if they're not careful, they might even get worse and risk their life in the process.

Elisabeth Elliot is one of my role models and all-time favorite writers. Her first husband, Jim, died as a martyr while spreading the gospel in Ecuador. Left with a six-month-old baby to raise on her own, Elisabeth was thrown into the Cherith of desperate need. She penned these words of prayer in *Keep a Quiet Heart* that should be our daily plea too: "God . . . calm me down, make me shut up and look to [You] for the outcome. His message to me every day [is to] wait, be still, trust, and obey."

God sent His Son to die on the cross for our sins. We've been given hope no matter what we're facing. God's Word is near us; His presence is in us. We have the ability to love the unlovable, to rejoice in suffering, to give though we're poor. The amazing and awesome power of God gives us victory over sin and the ability to overcome the toughest obstacles. It's been said that the Christian life is impossible. It is—if you try it on your own—but through the Holy Spirit living in you it is more than possible. It's time we settle down and slow down and recognize that God is at work in our midst even when we don't see Him clearly. Too many of us have missed God's work in our lives in our search for something "bigger."

The awesome thing about God is that He's a God of second chances. You might have tried arguing with Him and fighting for your way. You're exhausted and frustrated. Your life doesn't look like you think it should look. Your trust is shaky at best. You're living in the midst of chaos and you're not sure there's anything you can do about it. There is. While you might not be able to slow your life down as much as you'd like, now is the time to slow down your soul and listen. What is it that you need to surrender to the Lord? Perhaps it's your idea of perfection. You will find that there's power in yielded surrender. You might even see fire come down from heaven, or at least catch a glimpse of a bird with a loaf of bread in its beak. Wherever and however God chooses to reveal Himself to you, I guarantee that you'll notice Him best when you're quiet.

As we reach the end of our journey together, won't you resolve to find rest even in the midst of your chaos? It's more than possible. It's yours in Christ right now.

RESOLVED: that I won't let the hectic pace of the culture steal the peace that is mine in Christ but instead allow Him to speak to me in the middle of my busyness, knowing that I will find rest for my soul when I yield to Him in quiet surrender.

Conclusion

So Now What?

Now that you've committed to living by resolve, what should you expect? Where do you go from here? We're in that part of the book where we're about to say goodbye. It's time to wrap things up. I love being an ER doctor. I appreciate every aspect of my job, but I want to let you in on a little secret: no matter how much I love what I do, the best part of my ER shift is the end of it. I typically use the drive home from the ER to reflect over the day and replay its highlights. I evaluate where I need to change and consider how I need to improve. The beauty of working in the ER is that every shift is a new day, a new opportunity to do better.

It's very similar to the Christian life: every day brings new mercies. God's faithfulness is new every morning. I don't want to put too much pressure on you, but if you walk away from this book unchanged, then I've failed miserably.

Sometimes I get a kick out of my patients. I'll sit down with them and explain in simple English what their diagnosis is and how we're going to treat them. They nod their head and seem to follow what I'm saying. They look happy and satisfied. Right after I leave, the nurse walks in and tells them the exact same thing I just finished telling them. For example, she'll say, "You've got a broken bone." The patient will look up in shock and ask, "A broken bone? What are you talking about? Who has a broken bone?"

Life is funny that way. You can hear something once, twice, or three times and still not fully get it. That's why you've got to hear it from many different people and in many different ways. You might have already heard every principle I've shared in this book before, but you still catch yourself living your life shaken, fearful, and ineffective. I hope that's about to change. I hope I've been able to communicate the message of living with power in a way that has you going "Aha!"

Living by resolve is not a onetime, fix-all program. You can't do it all at once. Growth happens precept upon precept, line upon line, here a little, there a little (Isa. 28:13). Your walk with Christ is a daily exercise that you must fight for. Covet your time with God and protect it. The impact you will make in this life is in direct proportion to the depth of your relationship with Christ. Your life began when the unstoppable God reached down and grabbed you out of the pit. He is a God who is resolved about His love for you! He saw you and knew you and consecrated you before you were even conceived (Jer. 1:5). He understands you inside and out. He gets all of your idiosyncrasies and knows about your failures, but He's also the One who created you with your gifts and talents and amazing personality. He's not about to give up on you. He's in it for the long haul with you. He holds you by your right hand. He's for you and not against you. He is the One who will never forget you, never leave you, and never forsake you. He never sleeps nor slumbers and He never loses track of you (Ps. 121:4). He is steadfast. He loves you with unstoppable resolve. That's why He put on flesh and bones and came to earth in human form. His love for you is deep enough to die for you. He longs to be one with you, and prayed about this for you (John 17). But even more amazingly, after Jesus died and ascended to heaven, He sent us the Holy Spirit to take over and give us an even deeper form of intimacy with our God. Every detail of our lives now hinges on His abiding presence. Don't let anything get in the way of the transforming work of God in your life. Don't settle for comfortable and easy. Don't be satisfied with less than God's best for you.

When all of the things we've talked about in this book start falling together, your life will take on new power. Motivational speakers talk about "unleashing the power within" and "living out your destiny." I am not great at big words, but I do promise you that when God's Spirit takes over your life and you fix your all on the Lord, you will no longer be driven by your fears. You will no longer be miserable. When that happens, everyone will take notice.

Life is not as complicated as we make it out to be. Jesus died for us and He lives for us. Now it's time we wake up and live for Him with everything we've got. When you live like you believe what you say you believe, and when you stand strong in the heat of the battle, you're going to change your world. You're going to make a difference.

And this is how we do it.

Lina AbuJamra is a pediatric ER doctor and the founder of Living with Power Ministries. She loves Jesus and spends most of her time communicating biblical truth for everyday life through her popular blog and also through her speaking ministry, which has taken her all over the world. Her *Living with Power* podcast has more than 150,000 listeners from all over the world. She is also the host of *Today's Single Christian*, heard daily on Moody Radio.

LINA ABUJAMRA
Doctor. Author. Bible Teacher. Living With Power.

CONNECT WITH LINA AT
LIVINGWITHPOWER.ORG

🐦 @LinaMay

📷 LAbujamra

f Facebook.com/LivingWithPower

LISTEN TO LINA AT
TODAY'S SINGLE CHRISTIAN
ON MOODY RADIO

 **BakerBooks**
a division of Baker Publishing Group
www.BakerBooks.com

Available wherever books and ebooks are sold.

LIKE THIS
BOOK?
Consider sharing it with others!

- Share or mention the book on your social media platforms. Use the hashtag **#IAmResolved**.

- Write a book review on your blog or on a retailer site.

- Pick up a copy for friends, family, or strangers! Anyone who you think would enjoy and be challenged by its message.

- Share this message on Twitter or Facebook. **"Don't miss @LinaMay's great new book Resolved! #IAmResolved at LivingWithPower.org //@ReadBakerBooks"**

- Recommend this book for your church, workplace, book club, or class.

- Follow Baker Books on social media and tell us what you like.

 Facebook.com/ReadBakerBooks

 @ReadBakerBooks